# Nineteenth-Century Lights

## Historic Images of American Lighthouses

J. Candace Clifford

Mary Louise Clifford

Cypress Communications
ALEXANDRIA, VIRGINIA

Printed in the United States by Thomson-Shore, Inc., Dexter, Michigan

10      9      8      7      6      5      4      3      2      1


Library of Congress Catalog Card Number 99-75177

ISBN (softcover) 09636412-3-9
ISBN (hardcover) 09636412-2-0

Front cover illustration: *Gay Head Lighthouse built in 1856 on Martha's
Vineyard in Massachusetts (late 1880s photograph by Baldwin Coolidge courtesy
of the Society for the Preservation of New England Antiquities)*

Back cover illustration: *Seven Foot Knoll Lighthouse built in 1855 at the
Patapso River mouth on the Chesapeake Bay near Baltimore, Maryland (1885
photograph by Major Jared A. Smith courtesy of The Mariners' Museum, Newport
News, Virginia)*

Jacket and cover design by Dean Bornstein, The Perpetua Press, Barnet, Vermont

Published by      Cypress Communications
                  35 E. Rosemont Avenue
                  Alexandria, VA 22301
                  email <cypress@vais.net>
                  web address <http://www.vais.net/~cypress>

# CONTENTS

*Station survives but with a more recent lighthouse
**No lighthouse survives

# INTRODUCTION

Lighthouses are unique structures. They were built for utilitarian purposes, but we see them now as landmarks, monuments to the stalwart individuals who kept them, symbols of a more heroic era. Added to their innate appeal are the dramatic settings in which they are located. Whether the seas and rivers they lit are stormy or serene, their images grace countless paintings, vacation snapshots, tourist merchandise, poems, songs, movies, and logos.

This book presents nineteenth-century images of lighthouses, primarily photographs taken in the second half of the nineteenth century. The photos are arranged chronologically according to the year the tower in the photo was first illuminated. The date the photo was taken may not be known.

Building technology evolved at a rapid pace during the nineteenth century. The earliest towers were built of rubblestone or wood. Soon brick became a popular building material; later, cast iron was used. Toward the middle of the century towers were built offshore using screwpile and, later, caisson foundations. Some of the most amazing engineering feats were "wave-swept" lighthouses constructed with the use of offshore masonry cribs. Not until after the turn of the century was a reinforced concrete lighthouse constructed.

The federal government's establishment and management of aids to navigation paralleled the expansion of the United States into an international power. An association of colonies with locally mandated lighthouses grew into a nation with an integrated national system of lighthouses. By the end of the nineteenth century, the United States had the most extensive system of lighthouses in the world.

The sheer number of lighthouses constructed is amazing. We started the nineteenth century with 26 lighthouses and began the twentieth century with 1,228 "lighthouses and lighted beacons." Of these, some 650 appear to have been light stations with a resident keeper. [1] Today approximately 600 historic light stations survive, embracing all types of construction and materials. Many no longer serve as active aids to navigation but have been adapted as museums; national, state, and local park exhibits; wildlife refuges; inns; research facilities; and private homes. Many have been leased or transferred to groups that oversee their continued preservation. Almost half are accessible to the public.

Most of the images in this volume were taken by employees of the U.S. Light-House Board beginning in the 1850s. No photographers' names were associated with prints until the 1880s; two lighthouse engineers, Major Jared A. Smith and Herbert Bamber, are credited with many of the photos taken between 1880 and 1900. Most of the images selected are from the collections at the National Archives Still Pictures Branch in College Park, Maryland, or the U.S. Coast Guard Historian's Office, Washington, D.C. Many thanks to Robert Browning and Scott Price for their assistance in accessing the collection at the U.S. Coast Guard Historian's Office. The lighthouse plans are from the collection at the National Archives Cartographic Division in College Park, Maryland.

Textual records of the U.S. Lighthouse Service are housed at the National Archives, Washington, D.C., as Record Group 26. Archivists Rick Peuser, John VanDereedt, Rebecca Livingston, and the late Angie VanDereedt provided valuable assistance in pulling these records.

Thanks also to Susannah Livingston for her fine copyedit of the manuscript, Wayne Wheeler for his review, and Dean Bornstein for printing advice and cover design.

# I. Lighthouses in a New Nation

Through the ninth act of Congress in 1789, the federal government took control of the 12 colonial lighthouses then in operation.[1] In 1790 Congress authorized the nation's first public works project—the construction of the Cape Henry Light Station at the entrance to the Chesapeake Bay in Virginia. At first, lighthouses were constructed in response to local needs; later, as a system of aids to navigation developed, coastwide patterns evolved.

Most of the early lighthouses were concentrated in New England—the hub of commerce and industry—with the sailing ship the principal mode of transporting goods. The rocky coastline and numerous offshore shoals and islands required aids to navigation to protect the seaborne traffic. Of the 14 lighthouses built between the end of the Revolution and 1799, all but four were located north of New York City.[2] Of the 26 lighthouses built between 1801 and 1820, all but six were north of Delaware Bay.[3] Between 1821 and 1825, at the start of Stephen Pleasonton's tenure as superintendent of lighthouses, 29 more lighthouses were erected.

The construction of lighthouses was increasing in other parts of the world as well. There were an estimated 34 lighthouses worldwide in 1600, 66 lighthouses in 1700, and 175 lighthouses in 1800. In 1819 this number increased to 254; 52 of those were in the United States.[4]

The first American lighthouses were built of the materials that were readily available: wood and rubblestone. Because wooden towers burned or deteriorated at a greater rate than masonry in the harsh marine environment, few early examples survived into the age of photography. The wooden towers were generally framed into the roof of the keeper's dwelling. These towers were not supported by studs and consequently they often shifted in storms, causing leakage.[5] Although wood was America's most popular building material, sawn lumber was not available until the end of the eighteenth century and machine-made nails did not appear until the 1830s. Until that time, the wooden skeleton had to be assembled using mortise-and-tenon and pegs.[6]

The early masonry towers were built separately from the keeper's quarters, and were usually conical or octagonal in shape. The New England towers were generally built on a foundation of natural rock, using rubblestone split from the adjacent ledges or cliffs or collected on the beach. A lime and sand mortar was used to fill the cracks. The masonry towers varied in height from 20 to 50 feet; the walls were usually three feet thick at the base, tapering to two feet in thickness at the top. A brick dome was placed on the top of the tower and an iron and glass lantern (which shielded the lamps) was attached to the tower by imbedding the lower ends of its iron angle-posts into the masonry walls.[7]

The early nineteenth-century stations consisted of the light tower, a dwelling, a garden site, a place to store whale oil, a system to provide water, and maybe a chicken house and shelter for a milk cow. By mid-century, with the introduction of the more sophisticated Fresnel lens[8] and the fog signal (particularly the steam-driven siren or trumpet), the increased complexity of the operation required more personnel, who in turn needed additional housing and other support buildings. During the first half of the nineteenth century, keeper's dwellings generally had rubblestone walls, shingled roofs, and brick chimneys; the first floor divided into three rooms, and the second or attic floor contained three more small chambers. Keepers frequently complained of "smoky chimneys" over the lamps; ceilings were often black from soot. Cylindrical wooden tanks secured with iron hoops were located in the cellar to collect rainwater from the roof. Wells offering spring water were not common. Some offshore stations had to bring water from the mainland in casks.[9]

Many stations included a boat, generally small clinker-built canoes or common flat-bottomed dories. These were used primarily for transporting people or supplies, but they also enabled rescues of shipwrecked seamen or assistance to vessels in distress. The boathouse was generally a shed; the boat ways were "sticks of timber laid parallel to each other, extending from the boathouse to low-water mark, and secured to the rocks by iron stays."[10]

Windows were handmade, with muntins separating the panes of glass. The double-hung window was introduced around 1700. At the beginning of the nineteenth century, window panes were small, measuring 6 by 10 inches. The glass size increased as glass-making techniques improved. In the 1840s, the standard pane size was 8 by 14 inches with the overall window measuring 28 by 62 inches. Until the mid-nineteenth century, glass often contained bubbles and was not always clear.[11]

The candles used in colonial times were replaced by flat-wick lamps burning whale oil. Early models smoked dreadfully and were soon replaced by whale oil lamps with a hollow, circular wick that gave off much less acrid smoke. They were hung on a chandelier in front of parabolic reflectors that magnified the light. (Two different versions were named for their inventors, Ami Argand in Europe and Winslow Lewis in the United States.)[12] Shore lights were difficult to distinguish from one another; most lights were fixed, but some revolved by clockwork with a few colored or multiple lights for further distinction. In 1852 the proportion of revolving to fixed lights was 1 to 9.2.[13] According to the 1849 *Light List*, 11 stations had twin towers with twin lights and one station had three lights, but some mariners complained that these lights blended together when viewed at certain angles. They were later discarded for less expensive methods of classification.

During the second decade of the nineteenth century, a greater emphasis was placed on erecting lighthouses south of Delaware Bay. The southern shores of the United States are for the most part low and sandy, requiring tall towers if the light is to be visible to ships at sea. Although considerable commerce flowed through southern ports, a system of aids to navigation developed more slowly along the South Atlantic. In part this may have been because the South, with a largely agrarian economy, did not have a large ship-owning or merchant element agitating for better aids to navigation.[14]

The development of a system of lights on the Great Lakes came with the expansion of shipping and settlement. Construction of lighthouses was not only parallel to the growth in commerce; it was a prerequisite to that growth. One of the first lights on the Great Lakes was at Fort Niagara on the Niagara River connecting Lake Erie with Lake Ontario, completed in 1818.

During the period between 1792 and 1802, the Commissioner of the Revenue within the Treasury Department oversaw all work in connection with lighthouses. Between 1802 and 1813, the Secretary of the Treasury personally directed lighthouse activities, with the Commissioner again being reassigned the lighthouse duties between 1813 and 1820.

According to a law written in 1809, all lighthouses were to be built by contract, after advertising for proposals. The lowest bid was selected unless the bidder was found to have previously deceived the government. If the local collector could not oversee the work, he would appoint an "overseer" to monitor the progress of the job. The overseer was paid three dollars a day; the contractor would not be paid until the overseer certified that the job had been "faithfully done." The 1809 law also required the Lighthouse Establishment to advertise for proposals for obtaining oil and supplies.[15]

The early contracts to build lighthouses contained minimal instructions, generally little more than a sketch of the desired structure and a page of specifications. Appropriations for lighthouses were not generous; costs were to be kept at a minimum. Winslow Lewis, a contractor for many of the early lighthouses, reported his experiences to the Secretary of the Treasury in an 1843 letter:

> I have been the Contractor for building about 80 of our lighthouses. From 1817 to 1837 there was on our extended coast & Lake waters a rapid increase of Light houses. Petitions came to Congress from every quarter, the consequence was, the appropriations were extremely limited. In most instances from 4,000 to $6,000. In four instances 1,500, 1,600, 1,800 & $2,000 for the appropriation. The land was to be purchased, light & dwelling house built & the lighting apparatus to be paid for. Whenever I was called to give a plan I was confined to the limits of the small appropriation. This Sir, accounts for so many of your 2nd class of lighthouses not being built with more expensive & permanent materials. . . . a Light house built with hammered Granite dispensing with all wood, would be more durable than one built of brick or rubble stone with wood interior.[16]

Not surprisingly, many of the surviving early towers were modified over the years to increase their height for better visibility or to accommodate improved optics. Others were destroyed in natural disasters or events related to the Civil War. Often the materials of earlier obsolete towers were recycled for use in newer towers or other structures on the station.

# Sandy Hook Light Station (1764)

Of those lighthouse towers built before the Revolution, only one survives today: Sandy Hook Lighthouse located on the New Jersey shore at the entrance to New York Harbor. Constructed of rubblestone in 1764, the 85-foot tower was financed by New Yorkers through several lotteries and maintained through a tonnage tax collected from passing ships. Used by the British as a base for raids on Americans during the Revolution, the tower survived efforts by the patriots to destroy it. In 1852 the Light-House Board reported that it was one of the three best masonry lighthouses in the United States. The longest continuously operating lighthouse in the United States, Sandy Hook is now a National Historic Landmark located in a national park. (National Archives #26-LG-15-1)

# Boston Harbor Light Station (1783)

The need for an aid to navigation at the entrance to Boston Harbor was first recorded in 1701. On September 17, 1716, the *Boston News-Letter* contained the followed item:

> By virtue of an Act of Assembly made in the First Year of His Majesty's Reign, For Building & Maintaining a Light House upon the Great Brewster (called Beacon-Island) at the Entrance of the Harbour of <u>Boston</u> [*sic*], in order to prevent the loss of the Lives & estates of His Majesty's Subjects; The said Light House has been built; And on Fryday last . . . the Light was kindled, which will be very useful for all Vessels going out and coming in to the Harbour of <u>Boston</u> [*sic*], or any other Harbours in the Massachusetts-Bay, for which all Masters shall pay to the Receiver of Impost, One Peny [*sic*] per Ton Inwards, and another Peny Outwards, except Coasters, who are to pay Two Shillings each, at the clearance Out. And all fishing Vessels, Wood Sloops, etc., Five Shillings each by the Year.

This first lighthouse in the American colonies was actually constructed on Little Brewster Island and apparently constructed of stone. Light was provided at first by candles and later by lamps using fish oil. In 1720 a fire necessitated extensive repairs. In 1734 the wood lantern was replaced by a metal one and the tower was encased in wood. In 1751 another fire almost destroyed the structure.

The British took control of the light in 1774, then blew up the tower when they evacuated Boston in 1776. The Senate and House of the Commonwealth of Massachusetts ordered it rebuilt. A 75-foot tower with octagonal lantern was in operation in 1783 and has operated ever since. (Sandy Hook is the only tower in the United States older than the 1783 tower in Boston Harbor.)

In 1859 the 14 lamps used from 1839 until 1859 were replaced by a second-order Fresnel lens. The original fog signal was a cannon. A fog bell was commissioned in 1851; it was replaced by a compressed-air reed trumpet in 1872 and a steam siren in 1887. In 1859 the tower was extended in height to 89 feet as it appears on the next page.

Boston Harbor Light Station, a National Historic Landmark, is the only station in the country still manned by resident Coast Guard keepers, as required by Congress in a special act to commemorate its historical significance. (National Archives photo on next page from RG 26, Entry 17J)

# Montauk Point Light Station (1797)

> Montauk Point, at the east end of Long Island . . . is passed by all vessels approaching Long Island sound from seaward, and is a good point of departure for those leaving the sound. It is also frequently made by vessels from the southward bound to the northward and eastward, and by those approaching New York bay from the eastward.[17]

The historic tower on Montauk Point (drawing below) was authorized by George Washington and built by John McComb, son of a well-known architect and himself one of our country's famous early builders and architects. His contract stipulated that McComb erect an 80-foot tower of "Chatham freestone, fine hammered."[18]

In 1807 the local lighthouse superintendent wrote the Secretary of the Treasury that the assistant keeper at Montauk, Josiah Hand, had at his own expense installed a new type of lamp as an experiment. The superintendent visited the lighthouse and reported that the new light consumed much less oil than the old, gave a much brighter light because the wicks burned directly over the oil, and required less frequent trimming of the wicks. He was convinced that the lamp was a valuable innovation and that Keeper Hand deserved to be compensated for his expenses in installing the lamp.[19]

The 1839 *Light List*[20] recorded that the Montauk Point light tower displayed a new lighting apparatus in 1838: 18 lamps with 14 ½-inch parabolic reflectors arranged around two iron tables—ten on the upper and eight on the lower. Nearby stood three dwellings, one of which was badly deteriorated.

A VIEW OF THE
Light House on Montauk Point

The height of the tower was increased 17 feet in 1860 to accommodate a first-order lens. This drawing indicates where the new lantern and lens were placed upon the old tower. Montauk Point is still an active aid to navigation, with a museum in the keeper's dwelling. (National Archives drawings from RG 26)

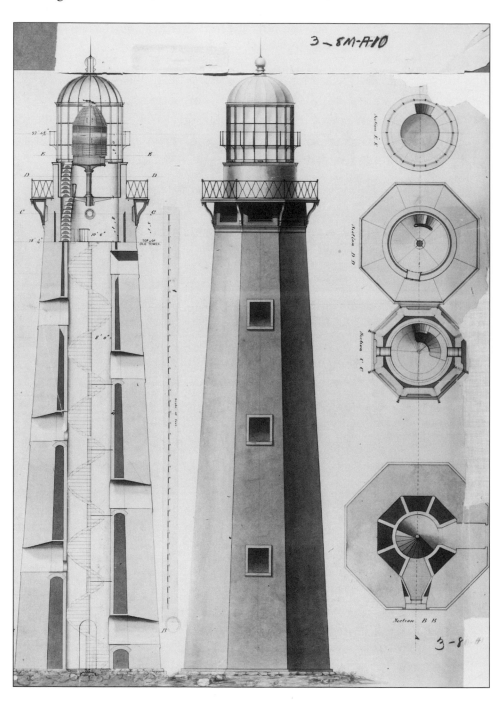

## Old Point Comfort Light Station (1802)

The steady flow of vessels through Hampton Roads in Virginia made aids to navigation essential. The first light at Old Point Comfort was established before the Revolution by a private caretaker, John Daines (or Dames, Danes), at Fort George, a strategic spot where the James River empties into Hampton Roads. The octagonal sandstone tower built by the federal government in 1802 on the north side of the James River mouth is the second oldest light station on the Chesapeake Bay.

A letter dated November 22, 1806, from the Norfolk collector to the Secretary of the Treasury, points up the problems of using whale oil lamps in early lighthouse lanterns:

> On the 19th instant about 12 o'clock at night the top of the lamp being much worn & not fitting close caused the oil to take fire & destroy 20 [?] or so panes of glass; the lamp is non repairing & I have directed the glass to be put in, which Mr. Luke the keeper can do himself & by tomorrow night I expect it will be lighted. I believe the keeper to be very attentive & that the accident did not happen to carelessness; he has . . . good lights & made it a rule to visit & fill the lamp with oil at midnight. I beg leave to sugest [sic] to you that if a large lanthorn [sic] was allowed at each Lt house with a box of candles in cases of the glass being broke by any means, it could be hung up & probably save the lives

of the crews and cargoes of some vessels in bad weather that run in expectation of seeing lights . . .[21]

The station was briefly captured and used as a lookout station by the British during the War of 1812. Construction of Fortress Monroe on Old Point Comfort began in 1819. A fourth-order lens was installed in the 1850s. From 1857 to 1861 this station had a woman keeper, Amelia Deweese (or Dewess).[22] The station was held by federal troops during the Civil War. In 1862 the federal keeper witnessed the battle between the USS *Monitor* and the CSS *Virginia* (ex-USS *Merrimack*), which took place on March 9 just offshore.[23]

The Old Point Comfort tower and Victorian-style wood-frame dwelling (rebuilt in 1891) still stand in the army base. The light is an active aid to navigation while the dwelling is used as officer's quarters. (1885 photo on previous page by Major Jared A. Smith courtesy of The Mariners' Museum, Newport News, Virginia)

## New Point Comfort Light Station (1804)

Using the same tower design as the Old Point Comfort Lighthouse (1802) but a few feet taller, the New Point Comfort Lighthouse was constructed of sandstone in 1804 on the eastern end of the Middle Peninsula in Virginia at the entrance to Mobjack Bay to serve traffic going up and down the Chesapeake Bay. Its first keeper was the man who built both the Old and New Point Comfort Stations, Elzy Burroughs of Mathews, Virginia.

In the 1840s a retired sea captain became keeper, assisted in 1852 by "a negro woman of his own."[24] Disabled by Confederates, the light ceased operation during the Civil War. Relit after the war and provided with a new lens, the light remained active until the 1950s, when it was replaced by a lighted buoy.

The keeper's dwelling was taken down in 1919. Harsh weather and hurricanes washed away the sand bar that connected the light station to the mainland. Local Mathews County organizations have banded together to raise money and preserve the light. Today the tower stands alone on a tiny riprap island a few dozen feet from the nearby sandy point. (1885 photo opposite by Major Jared A. Smith, National Archives #26-LG-23-30)

# Scituate Light Station (1811)

When established on Cedar Point in 1811 to guide ships into the harbor at Scituate, Massachusetts, the Scituate Lighthouse was a granite octagonal tower. The first keeper, Simeon Bates, spent considerable time away from the station, leaving his wife and nine children to assume his duties. Legend has it that during the War of 1812, Bates's daughters Rebecca and Abigail frightened away an enemy long boat by playing a fife and drum, pretending they were a marching militia.[25]

A brick addition raised the tower 15 feet in 1827 and supported a new lantern. The station was decommissioned twice with the completion of both the 1850 and 1860 Minots Ledge towers offshore. In each instance local citizens protested. A letter from a congressman in 1861 referred to "petitions from about six hundred citizens of several towns on Massachusetts Bay engaged in navigation, asking that the Light at Scituate harbor, which for a half a century has been a guide to the mariner . . . be restored."[26] A Fresnel lens was installed in the mid-1850s. With the Fresnel

lens in place in the lantern, the image on the previous page shows the station before it was decommissioned in 1860. Today the station is under the care of the Scituate Historical Society, its exterior restored to its 1830s appearance. (Photo opposite page courtesy of the USCG Historian's Office)

## Georgetown Light Station (1812)

One of the earliest federal lighthouses in the southeast was established in 1801 near Georgetown, South Carolina, on the east side of the entrance to the Peedee River. The brick tower shown here was built in 1812, refitted with a fourth-order lens in 1855, discontinued in 1861 because of the Civil War, and reestablished in 1867 with a new lantern and the new frame keeper's dwelling. An oil house was constructed in 1890, a boathouse in 1894. Georgetown Light is still an active aid to navigation. (Ca. 1890s photo by Herbert Bamber, National Archives #26-LG-28-4)

# Race Point Light Station (1816)

The rubblestone tower constructed at a westerly point on Cape Cod, Massachusetts, was originally 20 feet high. Raised five feet with brick in 1845, the tower was refitted with a fourth-order Fresnel lens in 1855. As with many stations in the harsh New England climate, the tower was connected to the keeper's dwelling by a covered walkway. Shown here ca. 1860, this tower was torn down and replaced in 1876. (Photo courtesy of the USCG Historian's Office)

# Tarpaulin Cove Light Station (1818)

This light was built in 1818 on the west side of Tarpaulin Cove on Naushon Island of the Elizabeth Island group in Massachusetts. Both the conical tower and dwelling were built of rubblestone, although the plan included here shows a hexagonal tower of cut stone. Both the photo and plan show a birdcage lantern, a type used before Fresnel lenses were adopted.

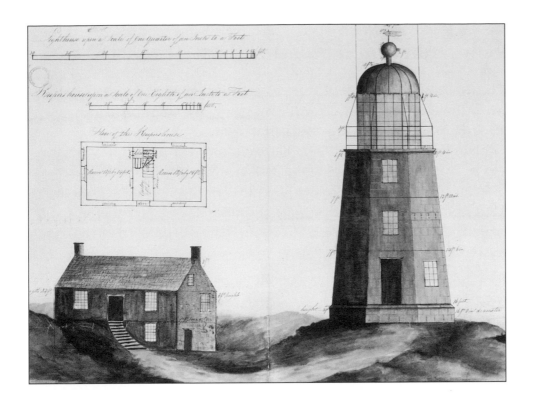

The house, although cheaply built, survived until 1888, when a frame house replaced it on the same foundation. The stone tower lasted until 1891, when it too was torn down and replaced by a brick tower and fourth-order lantern which survives today. (Above plan, drawn before 1818 construction, is from National Archives, RG 26; photo below courtesy of the USCG Historian's Office)

# Nantucket (Great Point) Light Station (1818)

The first keeper of the Great Point Lighthouse established on Nantucket, Massachusetts, in 1784 was a whaler named Captain Paul Pinkham, who achieved fame by publishing "A Chart of Nantucket Shoals Surveyed by Captain Paul Pinkham" in 1791. The wooden tower burned in 1816 and was replaced with a stone tower in 1818 at a cost of $7,385.12. A keeper's dwelling was added to the station in 1825. The tower was described in 1851 as constructed of "rough stone in courses, laid in lime mortar and a coat of cement on the outside."[27] A Fresnel lens was installed in 1857 and the tower lined with brick.

Its location badly eroded, the tower was destroyed in a 1984 storm; a replica of the old tower was built in 1986 with a five-foot-thick core of reinforced concrete at the bottom. (Photo of historic tower courtesy of the USCG Historian's Office)

## Bird Island Light Station (1819)

Built in 1819 on Bird Island, at the east entrance to Sippican Harbor off Buzzards Bay in Massachusetts, this lighthouse was constructed of rubblestone with lime mortar. In an 1851 report, the New Bedford collector indicated that the "mason work was very badly executed, the foundation has settled, and the wall bulged out on the easterly side, separating the outer part from the inner part of the wall two or three inches, several feet in circumference, the whole tower full of cracks and leaky . . ."[28] The collector suggested "that towers of Light Houses be constructed of stone laid in regular courses, with hammered joints, and the whole wall laid in cement—no lime mortar should be used."[29] He also recommended iron stairs and decks, since the wooden stairs were prone to rotting and the stone decks to leaking. (Photo courtesy of the USCG Historian's Office)

Legend has it that the first keeper, William S. Moore, was convicted of an unknown crime and sent to Bird Island without a boat as punishment. His wife tried three times to escape, so he killed her and buried her on the island. In 1853, the keeper was reportedly "addicted to drinking, gambling on the Sabbath, keeping disorderly house etc., and also that he was neglectful of his duties . . ."[30]

The drawing below shows the tower before it received a Fresnel lens in 1852. (Drawing from National Archives, RG 26) Note the indication of the early lamp and reflector system and the old-style lantern. The 1938 hurricane swept everything but the lighthouse off the island. The tower survives in 1999; the island is a nesting ground for endangered species.

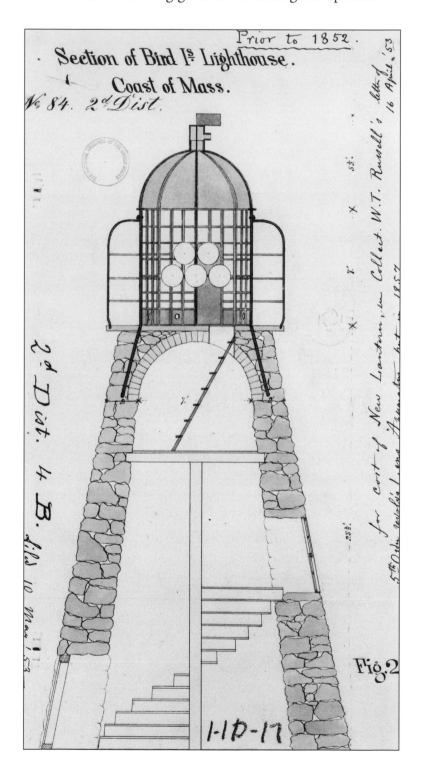

# II. Lighthouses Under the Fifth Auditor

The Secretary of the Treasury assigned the Fifth Auditor, Stephen Pleasonton, the "care and superintendence of the lighthouse establishment" between 1820 and 1852. The number of aids to navigation increased during this period from 55 lighthouses and a few buoys to 325 lighthouses and lightships[1] with numerous buoys and other aids to navigation.[2] Pleasonton's local representatives were the collectors of customs, also called superintendents of lighthouses, who selected sites and purchased the land for the lighthouses. They also supervised the contractors who erected the towers and related structures, and authorized repairs.[3] The captains of the local revenue cutters sometimes visited the lighthouses, providing Pleasonton with reports on conditions at the stations and the effectiveness of their lights in aiding navigation.

During the early years of the Republic, the United States lacked the resources to compete in trade with England or the rest of Europe. Not until after the War of 1812 was the United States able to catch up to and eventually surpass its competitors in using machine patents and technical discoveries and innovations. Financial growth and physical expansion were particularly explosive between 1820 and 1860. The Erie Canal was completed in 1825, linking the Great Lakes to the Hudson River and New York City. The expansion of the railroads linked to the Ohio-Mississippi river system extended the internal transportation system. Within a few years increasing shipments of grain, lumber, and coal flowed from West to East, and manufactured goods from East to West.[4]

Sandstone was used in several lighthouses built before 1800. After the turn of the century, granite became a popular choice for cut stone towers. Brownstone and limestone were used less frequently.

Brick was first used as a lining material for some colonial towers. After the turn of the century, it was used for the outer walls as well, especially in the southern states where stone was not readily available. Brick's small size, standardized production, and general availability soon made it the preeminent masonry material, although uncut stone continued in use where it could be obtained locally.[5] Although bricks of varying shades were manufactured in the United States, the Light-House Board felt that the strongest bricks were the ones with a reddish or reddish-gray color, derived from the iron oxide that abounds in the soil along the Atlantic coast.[6]

The first cast-iron-plate lighthouses were constructed in the early 1840s. James Rodgers completed a cast-iron tower for the Spanish government in Cuba before writing to Stephen Pleasonton suggesting that the proposed Sandy Hook Beacon be built of cast iron rather than wood. Rodgers cited the advantages of durability and strength, the ability to move the tower, roominess inside for the keeper, and resistance to fire.[8]

Funds could not be found to upgrade the Sandy Hook Beacon from wood to cast iron, so the first cast-iron-plate tower was built on Long Island Head, Boston Harbor, Massachusetts, in 1844 (drawing opposite). Because cast iron was lightweight (compared to brick and stone), inexpensive, strong, and watertight, and because it deteriorated slowly, cast-iron towers soon proliferated. A number of cast-iron towers were lined with brick for additional stability and insulation.

Iron (cast, wrought, or rolled) was used for lighthouse components such as stairs, galleries, railings, doors, shutters, door and window frames, and for joists, flooring, partitions, etc.[9] Cast iron was also used in the construction of skeletal towers, both offshore on screwpiles and onshore in locations where a relatively light structure was required to stand on mud, sand, swamp, or coral. Most were tubular towers consisting of a central vertical stairway cylinder with four to eight slanting skeletal supports. The components were prefabricated and tested offsite and easily reassembled on location. Cast iron was also found to be an excellent material for range and breakwater lights.

During the nineteenth century, the territories added to the U.S.—the Louisiana Purchase and Florida—did not require massive stone towers. With the acquisition of the Louisiana Territory in 1803, new ports were developed along the Gulf Coast. Along much of this coast, low, sandy islands were bordered by "extensive marshes, cut in all directions by lakes, bayous, lagoons, ponds, and sloughs, turning and twisting in every conceivable direction."[10] Protected anchorage behind the islands made aids to navigation

CAST-IRON LIGHT-HOUSE.

*Manufactured and erected on*

*Long Island Head, Boston Harbor,*

*by the South Boston Iron Company.*

*May 1844.*

ELEVATION.          SECTION. 2-2L-1

*Plans for the first cast-iron lighthouse, Long Island Head Light Station (1844), Massachusetts, from National Archives, RG 26*

crucial. The first lighthouses built along the Gulf of Mexico were copies of the sturdy New England brick towers; however, the softer soil of the Gulf Coast could not support the weight of these towers. Of the 40 or more constructed, 25 sank into the bottom or blew over, having no solid footing. By the 1840s, frame dwellings with the lantern mounted on top were used. These could be moved to escape erosion. Iron screwpile lighthouses were built along the coast before the Civil War. These offered a more stable foundation and could be built offshore, using a spiderlike cast-iron foundation below a wooden cottage-style dwelling supporting a lantern.[11]

Commerce sailing from New Orleans had to pass the Florida Straits to reach seaports in the East or in Europe, making this route one of the busiest in the world. In the Florida Keys ships were vulnerable to hazardous reefs as well as to piracy. Shipwrecks provided a lucrative trade to salvors or "wreckers."[12] Soon after Florida became a U.S. territory in 1821, Congress appropriated money to light the Keys. The first lighthouses built were Cape Florida, Key West Harbor, Sand Key, and Garden Key; a lightship was stationed at Carysfort Reef.[13] Florida Indians found isolated lighthouses easy targets for attack. Cape Florida was totally destroyed and one of its keepers killed in 1836.

Forty-three lights were in operation on the Great Lakes by 1840, including 17 on Lake Erie, 11 on Lake Michigan, nine on Lake Ontario, four on Lake Huron, one on Lake St. Clair, and one on the Detroit River. Thirty-three more, including six on Lake Superior, were introduced between 1841 and 1852.[14]

The quality of lighthouses built under Stephen Pleasonton left much to be desired. He took as much pride in saving money as in providing adequate aids to navigation. In 1843 Pleasonton wrote,

> I do not hesitate to say, that no similar establishment in the world now presents better lights, or is conducted with any thing like the economy. Being in possession of an official statement laid before Parliament in 1842, of the expenses of the British Lighthouses for 1840, I find the average was 3,602 dollars, whilst ours averaged 1,313 dollars only. This includes every expense of maintenance.[15]

In 1838, after being asked to authorize a number of new lighthouses, Congress appointed a board of navy commissioners to appraise the current lighthouse system and the need for or suitability of the proposed sites. The inspecting officers found that the quality of the nation's lighthouses ranged from very good to very bad. A number of poorly constructed towers led many of the inspectors to conclude that future construction should be supervised by a qualified engineer.[16] In 1845, two officers were sent to England and France to report on improvements in their lighthouse systems. Many of their recommendations were later adopted by the new Light-House Board. (Excerpts from their 1846 report can be found in the Appendix starting on page 273.) In 1847, after more complaints, Congress went so far as to assign the construction of six new lighthouses to the Army's Bureau of Topographical Engineers.

Although the 1838 reports of the commissioners noted structural flaws in many of the lighthouses, the most common flaw was in the quality of the light. The far superior French lenses had been alluded to as early as 1829 in a letter from Nathaniel Niles to Secretary of the Treasury Samuel Ingham. Reporting on the administration of lighthouses on the French coast, Niles wrote of "improvements made in the construction & lighting the lanterns. The old method of using reflectors [sic] has been renounced & a series of glass prisms or refractors [sic] substituted which are arranged as to throw all the light in a horizontal direction . . ."[17]

These complex lenses had prisms at top and bottom to refract light to the center of the lens, where it was intensified by powerful magnification.[18] Pleasonton did not test the French-manufactured Fresnel lens until 1841. Although these lenses would require a large capital investment, they would be more durable then the current system and would save oil costs by reducing the number of lamps needed. Pleasonton took no further steps, however, to introduce them in this country. His reluctance to adopt the superior lenses may have been based on Winslow Lewis's assessment of the new technology. After visiting the "French Lenticular Lights" being tested at the twin Highland Lights at Navesink, Lewis reported,

> The whole apparatus taken together, exhibits a beautiful specimen of workmanship, but far more complicated than any opinion, I had formed, more particularly the Lamp and its appendages, are extremely complicated,—many of its parts are of so delicate a texture, as to require constant attendance—so liable is the machinery of the Lamps to get out of order & and being but one source of Light, that it requires two Keepers for each Lighthouse, to stand watch & watch through the night, & one skilful [sic] machinist, with workshop & tools . . .[19]

Blaming the shortcomings of the reflector system used previously at Navesink on the small panes of the lantern, Lewis concluded,

> As a Lantern fitted up with our large reflectors will produce a Light that can be seen from 30 to 35 miles, as far as any light can be useful to navigators—I doubt, if hereafter, it will be thought advisable, to go to the expense of the French Lenticular . . .[20]

In 1848, calculations for contracting a supply of oil to be used in the lamps, indicated that the 256 lights used a total of 2,670 lamps, requiring 72,120 gallons of oil.[21] Oil increased in price over the years. Each keeper was required to make quarterly reports as to how much oil was used in his or her tower. The collector prepared an annual statement of each preceding year specifying "quantity and kind of Oil on hand at its commencement; the quantity and kind of Oil received during the year; the quantity and kind consumed during the year; and the quantity and kind remaining at the close of the year; the character and condition of the Oil, when received from the Contractors."[22] In the late 1840s, government agents replaced contractors in supplying and servicing the lights.

Lanterns were gradually improved upon in the first half of the century. Early lanterns used thick sashes and small panes in order that "the Lanterns might not blow away in the time of severe storms."[23] In 1843, however, Pleasonton reported, based on experience, "that it does not require half the quantity of sash formerly used, and that we may dispense with half at least, and enlarge the panes any size, . . . sometimes 24 by 18 and sometimes 3 feet by 2 feet."[24] As the old lanterns became corroded and worn out, they were replaced with this newer design, which was found to be much more effective.

The Lighthouse Act of 1848 included provisions for the inspection by naval officers of any potential lighthouse sites receiving appropriations from Congress. The purpose of the inspections was to ascertain whether the light was necessary and whether the best site had been selected. Forty light stations were completed in 1849, bringing the total to 299 lighthouses and 40 light vessels. The average expense per light in 1849 was $1,150.43 based on the salary of the keeper, repairs, and the cost of oil.[25]

## Ten Pound Island Light Station (1821)

Established on Ten Pound Island in Gloucester Harbor, Massachusetts, in 1821, this light guided fishing vessels into their home port. The 20-foot-tall octagonal stone tower stood 45 feet above the high watermark. In 1833 the collector of Boston reported that the light at Ten Pound Island was "wretchedly kept. The windows of the Lantern very dirty. The reflectors black and oily, and the whole appearance indicating extreme inattention and slovenlings [*sic*]. I recommend that the Keeper, James Sayward, be removed, and that Amos Story of Gloucester be appointed . . ." The original tower was replaced with a brown conical tower in 1881. The image above shows the station sometime after the sixth-order Fresnel lens was installed in 1866. (Courtesy of the USCG Historian's Office)

# Genesee Light Station (1822)

This 40-foot-tall rubble limestone octagonal tower was erected in 1822 on a bluff overlooking the mouth of the Genesee River on Lake Ontario, New York. Ten Argand lamps and reflectors served until 1853, when a new lantern to house a fourth-order Fresnel lens was added. The photo was taken after the new brick keeper's dwelling was built in 1863 and before the lighthouse was discontinued and replaced with a pier light in 1881. (National Archives #26-LG-45-36) Owned by Monroe County, which leases the station to the Charlotte-Genesee Lighthouse Society, it is open to the public with a museum in the keeper's dwelling.

# Stratford Point Light Station (1822)

A shingle-frame construction, the Stratford Point Lighthouse was 23 feet tall and sat 53 feet above sea level at the mouth of the Housatonic River on Long Island Sound in Connecticut. An 1837 inspection report was very derogatory:

> This lighthouse is in the worst order imaginable—The oil was when I visited it dripping from the lantern nearly to the base—the copper of the lantern deck is ripped up in many places, allowing a free passage for the oil from the lamps, under which there are no drippings to catch it. There are the strongest indications of this lighthouse being kept in the most careless, and slovenly manner.[26]

Refitted for a fifth-order Fresnel lens in the late 1850s, the lantern was later adapted to a third-order. In 1864 a fog signal was installed, prompting a request for an assistant keeper at $200 per annum.[27] The 1873 *Annual Report of the Light-House Board*[28] reported a bell struck by machinery at intervals of 10 seconds for four blows; a pause of 30 seconds, and then the 4 blows repeated. The photo below shows the station after the erection of the bell tower in 1864 and before the erection of a new tower in 1881. (National Archives #26-LG-17-13)

The following is the list of lighthouses and the number of lamps associated with each as reported by the Treasury Department in calculating how much oil would be contracted for in the following year. The total number of lamps was listed as 871. Note that the list runs down the coast, from Maine, Massachusetts, Rhode Island, Connecticut, New York (including five on the Great Lakes in Western New York, Pennsylvania, and Ohio), Delaware, Maryland, Virginia, North Carolina, South Carolina, and Georgia, and ending with two on the Gulf Coast in Alabama and Louisiana

| | | | | |
|---|---|---|---|---|
| Portland Head | 13 | | Point Judith | 10 |
| Seguin | 14 | | New London | 9 |
| Whitehead | 5 | | Faulkners Island | 12 |
| Franklin Island | 7 | | Lynde Point | 7 |
| Wood Island | 10 | | Five Mile Point | 8 |
| Papamaquoddy | 7 | | Fayerweather Island | 8 |
| Boon Island | 7 | | Stratford Point | 10 |
| Petit Manan | 8 | | Sandy Hook | 18 |
| Pond Island | 9 | | Sandy Hook Beacons | 13 |
| Burnt Island | 10 | | Eatons Neck | 12 |
| Libby Island | 10 | | Sands Point | 11 |
| Portsmouth | 11 | | Montauk | 13 |
| White Island | 15 | | Little Gull Island | 14 |
| Boston | 14 | | Buffalo | 9 |
| Nantucket | 14 | | Galloo Island | 15 |
| Nantucket Beacon | 6 | | Oswego | 8 |
| Thachers Island (two lights) | 16 | | Genesee | 10 |
| Bakers Island (two lights) | 29 | | Presque Isle | 10 |
| Plumb Island (two lights) | 14 | | Sandusky | 13 |
| Cape Cod | 16 | | Cape Henlopen | 13 |
| Cape Poge | 7 | | Bodkin Island | 13 |
| Plymouth (two lights) | 12 | | North Point (two lights) | 18 |
| Wigwam Point | 5 | | Cape Henry | 14 |
| Chatham (two lights) | 14 | | Old Point Comfort | 10 |
| Scituate | 7 | | Smiths Point | 9 |
| Race Point | 10 | | New Point Comfort | 9 |
| Point Gammon | 7 | | Bald Head | 15 |
| Holmes Hole | 8 | | Cape Hatteras | 14 |
| Tarpaulin Cove | 7 | | Charleston | 10 |
| Bird Island | 10 | | North Island | 7 |
| Long Island Head | 10 | | Tybee | 15 |
| Ten Pound Island | 10 | | Tybee Beacon | 6 |
| Billingsgate Island | 8 | | St. Simons Island | 7 |
| Gayhead | 10 | | Wolf Island (two lights) | 12 |
| Clarks Point | 8 | | Cumberland Island | 14 |
| Cutter Hunk Island | 13 | | Mobile Point | 15 |
| New Port | 10 | | Franks Island | 30 |
| Watch Hill | 10 | | | |

# Black Rock Harbor Light Station (1823)

Established to guide large sailing vessels into the deep waters of the port at Black Rock Harbor, Connecticut, the station was located on the south end of Fayerweather Island. The 1823 tower replaced an earlier wooden tower demolished in a hurricane. This light was tended by Catherine Moore for 67 years. Moore said, "On [calm] nights I slept at home, dressed in a suit of boy's clothes, my lighted lantern hanging at my headboard and my face turned so that I could see on the wall the light from the tower and know if anything had happened." She walked across two wet, slippery planks to reach the tower and fix the lamps. She assisted her invalid father from 1817 until 1871, then acted as official keeper from 1871 until 1879. She also grew a huge garden; tended chickens, several sheep, and a cow; seeded and harvested oysters; carved duck decoys; and saved at least 21 lives.[30] (Ca. 1870 photo, National Archives #26-LG-11-3)

## Ocracoke Light Station (1823)

The first tower, built in 1803, was destroyed by lightning. In 1823, a 76-foot masonry tower with its one-story, three-room brick keeper's dwelling was located on the Outer Banks, North Carolina, near the village of Ocracoke. A fourth-order lens was installed in 1854, but was removed by the Confederates in 1861 or 1862. Returned to service in 1863 or 1864, the station remains active in 1999. The station is shown here in 1893 after a second floor was added to the dwelling in 1887. (Photo by Herbert Bamber, National Archives #26-LG-71-95)

## Sodus Point Light Station (1825)

Lake Ontario ship captains petitioned Congress in 1824 for a light to mark the entrance to Sodus Bay between Rochester and Oswego, New York. A rough split-stone tower and keeper's dwelling were constructed the following year. A Mr. Wickham sold part of his shore property to the federal government for the lighthouse, but then wrote several letters to the Lighthouse Establishment asking to retain his right to fish from what had been his land. The solicitor of the Treasury ruled in 1837 that light keeper Fitzhugh could take whatever steps necessary to keep Wickham off federal property. Wickham thereafter appealed unsuccessfully to his congressman to restore his fishing rights.

The first Sodus Point Light is shown here in 1858. The 1869 *Annual Report* states that only slight repairs were made to the soon-to-be-replaced tower. The new tower was completed in 1871. The old tower and house were razed and the material used for a 70-foot jetty to protect and build up the shoreline. (National Archives #26-LG-43-20)

# Owls Head Light Station (1826)

The building of ships and the burning and shipping of lime were important on the Maine coast early in the nineteenth century. Owls Head Light was established in 1826 on the west side of the entrance to Penobscot Bay overlooking Rockland Harbor in Maine. The short tower of whitewashed brick stood on a headland that put it 147 feet above sea level. The one-and-a-half-story wooden keeper's dwelling, painted brown, sat lower on the hill.

This early light had eight oil lamps with 15-inch reflectors. In 1853 it was refitted with nine lamps and 21-inch reflectors. A year later a new keeper's house was erected. In 1856 a fourth-order Fresnel lens replaced the reflectors. A small fog bell was added in 1869. Ten years later a bell operated by a Stevens Striking Machine was installed. A telephone connected the lighthouse with Owls Head village in 1898. An active aid to navigation, the station is accessible in Owls Head State Park. This photo was taken some time after the tower was refitted for a fourth-order Fresnel lens in 1856. (Courtesy of the USCG Historian's Office)

## Long Point Light Station (1827)

Long Point Light was established to mark Provincetown Harbor on Cape Cod Bay in Massachusetts, and is shown here after it was refitted with a Fresnel lens in the 1850s. The lighthouse was replaced with a square white tower with a black lantern in 1875. (National Archives #26-LG-7-36)

## Cove Point Light Station (1828)

Though a lightship was recommended by an inspector and supported by local captains and pilots, Cove Point Lighthouse was established in 1828 at the mouth of the Patuxent River in Maryland. (The lightship was seen as too costly by the Fifth Auditor.) The 38-foot tower and detached keeper's quarters were built by John Donahoo of Havre de Grace, using locally-manufactured brick for $5,685. Donahoo, a commercial fisherman and builder, built many of the early lighthouse towers on the Chesapeake Bay. The keeper lived in a 20- by 34-foot brick keeper's house, built on the design used at Thomas Point, Bodkin Island, North Point, Pooles Island, Havre de Grace, and Fog Point. A fifth-order Fresnel lens replaced 11 lamps with reflectors in 1855. The fog bell was struck by machinery. In 1883 the roof of the dwelling was removed and the walls raised to add a new upper floor with three rooms.

The fourth-order lens installed in 1897 continues as an active aid to navigation in the 1828 tower. (1885 photo on opposite page by Major Jared A. Smith courtesy of The Mariners' Museum, Newport News, Virginia.)

Cove Point Light Station

## Cape Elizabeth Light Station (1828)

An early piece of correspondence indicated the need for approaching mariners to be able to distinguish Cape Elizabeth from Richmond's Island. "Formerly a windmill stood on the cape which in some measure answered the purpose of a Beacon," but it had recently "decayed and is demolished."[31] The station at Cape Elizabeth, Maine, was established in 1828 with two rubblestone towers 300 yards apart, one equipped with a flashing light, the other with a fixed. The station used a fog bell until one of the first steam-operated fog signals was installed in 1867. This photo of the west tower was taken after a third-order lens was installed in the late 1850s and before the tower was given one broad vertical red stripe as a daymark in the mid-1860s. The rubblestone towers were replaced with two cast-iron towers lined with brick in 1873. (National Archives #26-LG-1-59)

## Back River Light Station (1828)

A lighthouse was constructed in 1828 at the mouth of Back River on the Chesapeake Bay, Virginia, about five miles northeast of Old Point Comfort. A footbridge spanned a marsh, connecting the tower and the keeper's dwelling. Neither the tower, shown on facing in 1885, nor the dwelling survives. (Photo opposite by Major Jared A. Smith courtesy of the USCG Historian's Office)

Back River Light Station

# Cape Romain Light Station (1828, 1858)

This photo shows two towers at Cape Romain, a light station established in 1828 on Raccoon Key on Cape Romain, about 10 miles southwest of the entrance to the Santee River in South Carolina. The aid is an important guide around shoals for ships bound for Charleston. The 1828 tower to the left was 65 feet high and still had the old birdcage lantern used when multiple lamps with reflectors were hung from a chandelier in the lantern. The tower to the right, completed in 1858, is a much taller (150 feet) first-class seacoast light built in the form of a frustum of an octagonal pyramid.

In 1862 the lens and lantern in this tower were destroyed. The light was reestablished in 1866, but the keepers' dwellings were leaking badly and needed new roofs. By 1873 the tower had settled on one side, putting it 23 ½ inches off vertical. Annual measurements indicated additional canting, but corrective measures were never taken. In 1886 the old tower was fitted up as an oil house by installing a fireproof door and laying a concrete floor.

The 1858 tower was deactivated in 1947 and survives along with the bottom third of the 1828 tower. Both are located in the Cape Romain National Wildlife Refuge. (Ca. 1890s photo by Herbert Bamber)

# Cleveland Harbor Light Station (1829, 1831)

A lighthouse was established in 1829 at the corner of Main and Waters Streets to serve the harbor at Cleveland, Ohio, augmented in 1831 with a beacon established on the end of the pier. In 1833 Keeper Stephen Woolverton wrote the director of the Lighthouse Establishment, asking that his $350 salary be increased by $100 a year (retroactive) for tending the beacon, which was three-quarters of a mile from the lighthouse on a pier often covered with ice. Stormy weather and high winds required the keeper's presence all night.

> The lamps must be trimmed or snuffed about twelve o'clock at night, and if [the keeper] come on shore, a sudden storm of wind could cause the sea to break over the pier, that he could not get to the beacon, and the lamps would go out before day. The beacon has not been a single night without a keeper in it during . . . the navigable season—it has been tended a part of the time by my son, a boy of sixteen years of age, and by another person whom I have hired.[32]

Fifth Auditor Pleasonton favored his request, but the Secretary of the Treasury permitted only a $50 increase. Woolverton, supported by the captain of the local revenue cutter, wrote again that he could not find a man to tend the beacon for less than $20 a month, which was putting him into debt. His salary was increased to $500 in 1834, but the collector of customs in Cleveland wrote the Treasury Secretary that the keeper at Grand River performed the same duties for only $400 per annum.

On December 18, 1837, Woolverton announced that he had invented a lamp superior to the Lewis lamp then in use. Although the fate of this new invention is not known, the descriptions do illustrate deficiencies in the lighting system then in place.

> My lamp is on a more simple, cheap, and durable construction than those now in use (called Winslow Lewises patent Lamp). . . .will make much more light . . . requires not tube glasses nor stones to keep the oil warm, in the coldest weather, will consume less oil, as it makes no drippings, and will burn from ten to twelve hours without requiring snuffing or trimming, whereas, W. Lewises lamp will not do well without snuffing every four hours; and it can scarcely be expected that all Light House Keepers, can at all times, snuff their lamps at the end of every four hours, if they do, they get very little rest through the night, and if they do not snuff at the end of four hours, they have a bad light . . .[33]

Woolverton echoed what must have been a common complaint from all keepers of the period when he wrote, "the lamps in use are very

Cleveland Harbor Light Station

LIGHTHOUSES UNDER THE FIFTH AUDITOR

complicated, though apparently in good order, will frequently refuse oil to the burner, and will go out in a few minutes; besides, the oil passes through long tubes, and unless the lantern is kept warm, the oil becomes cold in the tube, and the lamp goes out in a short time."[34]

In 1838, the Secretary of the Treasury received a complaint about the filthy condition of Woolverton's station. Edward Merrill reported that

# Point Lookout Light Station (1830)

Point Lookout Lighthouse, located on the north side of the Potomac River where it runs into the Chesapeake Bay in Maryland, was built in 1830 by John Donahoo, who had submitted the lowest bid of $3,350. Over a period of 26 years, from 1825 to 1853, Donahoo built 12 of the first 17 lighthouses in Maryland; seven remain standing. (Those that did not survive either succumbed to erosion or were torn down.)

James Davis was appointed Point Lookout's first keeper but passed away less than three months later. His wife, Ann, was appointed as his replacement with a salary of $350 per year; her contract forbade the selling of liqueurs on the station grounds. In 1840, Ann was complimented in a report by the captain of the lighthouse supply boat, who wrote, "Mrs. Davis is a fine woman, and I am sorry she has to live on a small naked point of land." Ann Davis served Point Lookout until her death in 1847. Two other women kept the light at Point Lookout: Martha A. Edwards from 1852 to 1855, and her daughter Pamela[36] Edwards from 1855 to 1869.

The Fifth auditor, Stephen Pleasonton, had no qualms about appointing female keepers to replace related male keepers who died in service. In 1851, he wrote,

> So necessary is it that the Lights should be in the hands of experienced keepers that I have, in order to effect that object as possible, recommended on the death of a keeper, that his widow, if steady and respectable should be app't to succeed him, and in this way some 30 odd widows have been appointed.[37]

The station was deactivated in the 1960s and is now part of the Patuxent Naval Air Station. (1883 photo by Major Jared A. Smith, National Archives #26-LG-24-5)

# Mount Desert Rock Light Station (1830, 1847)

The Mount Desert Rock Station was established 20 miles off the coast of Maine in 1830. The 1830 tower, shown in the National Archives drawings below and facing page, was reported in 1831 to have been badly built: "the material is all bad—the mortar in particular is made with salt water sand & mixed with salt water, if you can analyze it you can see no lime whatever . . . the dwelling house in bad order—leaks much—and smoaks [*sic*] badly."[38] The tower lasted only 17 years.

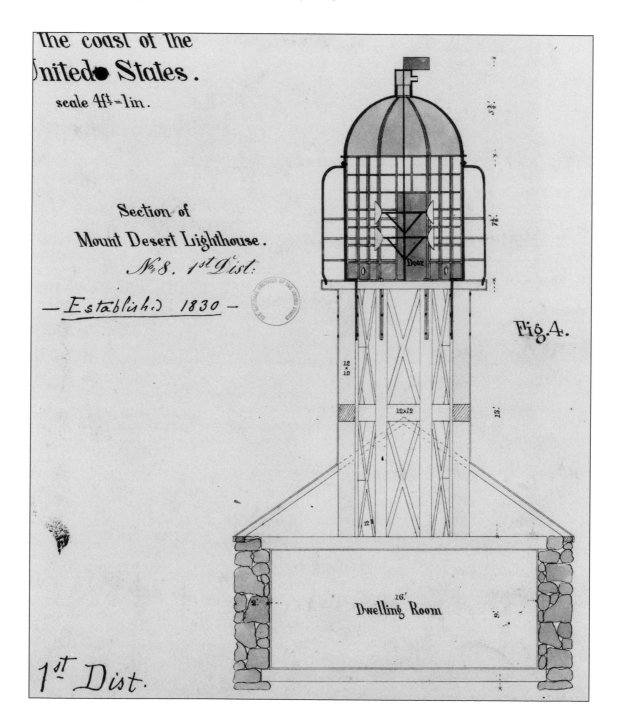

The coast of the
United States.
scale 4ft = 1in.

Section of
Mount Desert Lighthouse.
№ 8. 1st Dist.
— Established 1830 —

Fig. 4.

Door

Dwelling Room

1st Dist.

Fig.1.

Mount Desert Lighthouse. *N° 8. 1st List*
Coast of Maine.

Fig.3.

In an 1843 report regarding salaries at four Maine lighthouses—Mount Desert Rock, Matinicus Rock, Saddleback Ledge, and Boon Island—I.W.P. Lewis stated,

> These four places are lone rocks, standing several miles from shore—
> There is nothing but the naked barren rock & the lighthouses for the eye
> to rest upon—In storms the sea breaks furiously over the buildings & the
> keepers & their families are in danger of being swept away—Nothing can
> well be imagined more desolate & uncomfortable than such situation—
> All supplies of stores & fuel are necessarily obtained from the mainland
> during the summer season as these rocks are inaccessible during the fall
> & winter.[39]

The replacement tower made of "hammer-dressed" stone was designed by the noted architect/engineer Alexander Parris, who was commissioned to design at least five lighthouses in Maine. Mount Desert Rock was considered by some as the most exposed station in the United States. The image on page 47 was taken after the tower was raised 10 feet in 1857 to accommodate a third-order Fresnel lens. (Courtesy of the USCG Historian's Office) The image above shows the station after the clapboard double keeper's dwelling was constructed in 1893. (National Archives #26-LG-4-17)

# Cat Island and Pass Christian Light Stations (1831)

Mississippi Sound is sheltered from the Gulf of Mexico by a chain of islands extending irregularly from Mobile Point westerly as far as Cat Island. Cat Island was named by the French for the queer-looking animals with face masks—raccoons—that overran the place. Using identical plans, Cat Island and Pass Christian Lighthouses were built in 1831 on the Mississippi Sound (which borders Mississippi, Louisiana, and Alabama) to mark the approach to New Orleans. (Both photos courtesy of the USCG Historian's Office)

The construction contract calling for brick buildings was won by Winslow Lewis for $9,283. In 1843 the captain of the U.S. Revenue Cutter *Woodbury* described the Pass Christian Light to the Secretary of the Treasury as "a small tower of 30 feet on elevated ground, exhibiting a fixed light from eight lamps with reflectors. The location is good and the light very necessary to the security of the Coasting Trade and the transportation of the U. S. Mail by steamboats." The report continued, however, "the stairs of the tower are much decayed, and require immediate repair, the lantern is leaky, and also the lantern deck admitting the rain, to the injury of the lights, and damage of the wall; the dwelling house leaks badly in the roof, and the floors from their irregular giving way, indicate the rottings of

the sleepers. This rapid decay is owing to the floors being too near the ground, and without ventilation underneath."[40]

Shown on the previous page in the late 1850s, the tower on Cat Island was severely damaged by hurricanes in 1855 and 1860. Burned during the Civil War, the undermined tower was replaced in 1871 with an iron screwpile lighthouse, which no longer exists.

Pass Christian Light survived the Civil War, but the light was obscured by trees that had grown up on the adjacent property. When the owner of the trees refused to trim them, the Light-House Board decided to discontinue the light in 1882 and sell the valuable property, situated on the main street of the village.

## Buffalo Harbor Light Station (1833)

Established around 1819 and one of the earliest stations on the Great Lakes, the first Buffalo Harbor Lighthouse was seen as useless. The second lighthouse, made of hewn limestone and erected on a pier, was completed in 1833. The population of Buffalo quadrupled in the seven years after the opening of the Erie Canal in 1825; half were immigrants from overseas. The Buffalo Harbor Lighthouse welcomed these immigrants as they arrived in packet boats via the Erie Canal. Many stayed in Buffalo while others boarded steamers and packets to traverse the Great Lakes and establish communities farther inland.[41]

In 1857 the original lantern was removed and replaced with a course of stone casement windows, service room, and lantern to accommodate a third-order Fresnel lens. The old tower was reduced in importance as the harbor expanded outward, and was discontinued in 1914. Still under the jurisdiction of the U.S. Coast Guard in 1999, the property is licensed to the Buffalo Lighthouse Association. (National Archives photo from RG 26, Entry 17J, ca. 1857)

## Goat Island Light Station (1835)

A tower was constructed of rubblestone in 1835 on the north end of Goat Island to mark the narrow entrance to Cape Porpoise Harbor, Maine, considered the safest harbor between Portsmouth, New Hampshire, and Portland, Maine. (National Archives #26-LG-2-27) The light also warned vessels of hidden ledges. A "Journal of Shipwrecks at Goat Island," kept by the light's keepers from 1865 to 1920, records 46 vessels straying onto the rocks; of these, 28 were deemed a total loss. Fortunately no loss of life was reported among the 229 crewmen. The tower was replaced in 1859.

## Ashtabula Harbor Light Station (1836)

In 1836, a light was located on the extremity of the east pier forming the entrance to Ashtabula Harbor on Lake Erie in Ohio. The light is shown here after the lantern was renovated for a fifth-order Fresnel lens in 1859. In 1872 the *Annual Report* stated that "the beacon on the east pier is very old and dilapidated, and by the irregular settling of the crib has been much thrown out of vertically [*sic*]." An appropriation for a new beacon on the proposed extension of the west pier was made in 1873; the new lighthouse was completed and the old tower removed in 1876. (National Archives #26-LG-43-1)

Ashtabula Harbor Light Station

# Ipswich Light Station (1838)

The 1839 *Light List* describes two towers, 30 feet high, 500 feet from one another, at the south side of the entrance to Ipswich Harbor, Massachusetts. According to the 1869 *Light List*, the rear range was painted white and the front range black. In 1881, the main light was replaced with an iron tower. The front range was discontinued in 1932. Neither tower is known to survive.

Massachusetts was one of the first states concerned with providing lifesaving services along its coast. The Massachusetts Humane Society provided structures for volunteer rescue teams long before the federal government became officially involved with addressing the need for lifesaving stations. The need for a lifeboat at Ipswich was the subject of an 1840 petition signed by 80 "respectable citizens" and forwarded to the Secretary of the Treasury by the local collector. The petition read, in part,

> . . . many disastrous shipwrecks have lately occurred on the coast in this vicinity, whereby many valuable vessels have been destroyed, and many lives lost, and we have reasons to believe that if the neighboring lighthouses had been provided with life boats, the lives of many who have been lost, might have been preserved, we therefore pray that the light house in Ipswich may be provided with a life boat, & other apparatus for rescuing the shipwrecked mariner from peril & danger.[42]

(National Archives #26-LG-7-31)

## Ned's Point Light Station (1837)

The Ned's Point Light station, located on the northeast side of the entrance to Mattapoisett Harbor, Massachusetts, was established in 1837. An 1838 report discussed the deficiencies of the station:

> This light . . . consists of eleven lamps with thirteen-and-one-half-inch reflectors—six in the lower, and five in the upper tier. . . . a single common lantern, sufficiently elevated, would answer all the purposes . . ., whereas now between three and four hundred gallons of oil a year are being consumed. The lamps are so arranged that three of them are reflecting their light to no useful purpose towards the interior.

> I recommend that seven of these lamps be suppressed, and that remaining four be compactly arranged, so as to show the entrance to the harbor. . . .

> The tower and dwelling are of stone, and . . . have recently been erected. The keeper informs me that, in the late storm, both buildings leaked in all directions. The unskilfulness [*sic*] of the work extended to the lantern, the dome of which also leaked, rendering it prudent for the keeper to remain by the lamps during the rain, lest the light should be extinguished. I removed the surface of the mortar or cement, in several places, and found the stone to be laid in what appeared to be very little more than sand. The glazing of the lantern was to have been of Boston double-crown glass, but evidently glass of the thinnest kind has been used . . . I found the lantern to be only five feet eight inches high, which is too low, again, for the convenience of the keeper with his hat on.[43]

The keepers apparently worked with these deficiencies for two decades. A Fresnel lens was placed in the Ned's Point Light in 1857. In 1888 the dilapidated stone dwelling shown on the opposite page was torn down and a frame house built on its foundation. In 1896 the birdcage lantern and deck were replaced and a fifth-order lens installed. (Courtesy of the USCG Historian's Office)

---

## Eagle Island Light Station (1838)

A light station was established in 1838 on Eagle Island in East Penobscot Bay not far from Deer Island, Maine. The 1857 *Annual Report* stated that Eagle Island should be rebuilt; the report of the following year indicated, however, that a new lens had been installed, presumably requiring a new lantern as well. In 1879, two years after the illuminant was changed from lard oil to kerosene, keeper A.P. Sweetland complained, ". . . I have to hurry all the time cleaning, painting, white washing the dock and premises, building a fence to mark the garden. The light keeps me up nearly all night, it requires a great deal of care and watchfulness—to have a good light. I wish the L.H. Board would go back to lard oil."[44] (Courtesy of the USCG Historian's Office)

# Nantucket Cliff Range Lights (1838)

Aside from the Great Point Light marking the northern extremity of Nantucket Island, several other aids were built on Nantucket Island off the Massachusetts coast. A light on Brant Point and behind it a beacon formed a range to mark the entrance to the harbor. In 1838, two additional lights referred to as the Nantucket Cliff Range Beacons were built to mark the channel.

When two new beacons were built nearby, the keeper of the main light, David Coffin, offered to tend them for an additional $200 per year. The local collector supported his proposal, describing the distance between the old tower and the first of the two under construction as one-half mile over heavy beach sand, the new lights being one-quarter or one-third of a mile apart. "It is my opinion that an active man could keep all <u>three</u> [*sic*] Beacon lights, the keeper of the Beacon Light is rather in years, but I am decidedly of the opinion that it is best to have him to make tryal [*sic*] to keep the three."

Pleasonton rejected his proposal, saying the distance between the main light and the new beacons

> [render] it impossible in my opinion for one keeper to do justice to all the lights. Whilst in England they have two & three keepers for one Light House, and in France four keepers for each principal Light House, we could hardly expect one keeper would do full justice to the keeping of three lights and they are half a mile apart. The saving too would be one hundred dollars as the present keeper asks 200 dolls [*sic*] for attending the new lights and it would only be necessary to give three hundred dollars to new keeper.[45]

In 1851 the whitewashed wooden towers were 185 and 80 feet from shore; each contained one lamp with four tubes, without reflectors. The rear tower was about six feet taller than the front.[46] The first image shows the towers before 1889, when the front tower was rebuilt and the height of the rear tower increased (National Archives #26-LG-8-55); the second image was taken after these modifications. (National Archives #26-LG-8-56) Neither tower exists today.

# Tchefuncte River Light Station (1838)

Prosperous boatyards and health spas on the Tchefuncte River prompted calls for a lighthouse located where the Tchefuncte River emptied into Lake Pontchartrain, Louisiana. It was authorized by Congress in 1834, but construction was delayed until 1837 because of a clouded land title. Lighting of the tower was further delayed until the end of 1838 because the New Orleans customs collector forgot to contract for the lamps and reflectors. The tower is shown here soon after the old reflector system was replaced with a Fresnel lens in 1857. Damaged beyond repair in the Civil War, the tower was rebuilt on its old foundation in 1867 and is still extant. (Courtesy of the USCG Historian's Office)

## Mayo's Beach Light Station (1838)

In 1838, the Superintendent of Boston reported that the lighthouse on Mayo Beach, Wellfleet Bay, Massachusetts, was finished and ready for a keeper, although he was of the opinion that "it is of no use whatsoever." Despite reports that the Billingsgate Light already lit the entrance to Wellfleet Harbor, the Mayo's Beach Light Station served for 87 years. An earlier justification for the harbor light said another light was needed to guide ships through some "intricate navigation" of the seven miles between Billingsgate Point and the head of the harbor, elaborating, "that there are belonging to this port over one hundred vessels, employed in the coasting trade, and fisheries of from 25 to 100 tons—and the imports are considerable for the maintenance of the inhabitants, as the country back is sterile and unproductive."[47]

The aid to navigation at Mayo's Beach was described in the 1854 *Light List* as a "red tower, harbor light on keeper's dwelling." The tower shown was replaced with a cast-iron tower in 1880 and the station discontinued in 1925. (National Archives #26-LG-8-10)

## Saddleback Ledge Light Station (1839)

Saddleback Ledge Lighthouse was designed by Alexander Parris, a professional architect and engineer and a leading proponent of using granite as a building material. Constructed on the east side of the entrance to Isle au Haut Bay, Maine, in 1839, Saddleback was described in 1842 by I.W.P. Lewis, civil engineer, in his report to the Secretary of the Treasury on the condition of lighthouses in Maine, New Hampshire, and Massachusetts:

> . . . [It is] simply a conical tower of hammered granite, the base being sunk below the surface of the rock, and resting upon a level plane, quarried out for the purpose. The stones of each course are equal to the thickness of the wall, and the joints, being very close, are filled with hydraulic cement of pure quality. The sea breaks quite over the lantern in a southeast gale. The tower contains four apartments for the use of the keeper, but no convenience for collecting fresh water, nor any means for securing a boat—both important omissions. However, the cost of the work was but $15,000, and it is the most economical and durable structure that came under observation during the survey, and, what is worthy of special remark, the only one erected in New England by an "architect and engineer."[48]

(Courtesy of the USCG Historian's Office)

# Chatham Light Station (1841)

The twin wooden towers at Chatham, on southeast Cape Cod, Massachusetts, were replaced with brick towers in 1841. An 1843 report stated, "Chatham Light is intended and answers the purpose of guiding vessels past the shoals, either way, getting the light to bear NNW and running SSE carries clear of a dangerous shoal called Pollock Ripp, and also directs vessels from Old Stage harbour to Hyannis."[49]

After the change in administration in 1849, many keepers feared they would be replaced with political appointees supporting the new party in power. Chatham's keeper, Angeline Nickerson, feared for the loss of her livelihood. A letter written in her behalf to newly elected President Zachary Taylor pleaded her case:

> Upon the death of Mr. Simeon Nickerson the keeper of the "Chatham Lights," . . . in October Last, Mrs. Angeline Nickerson his widow was appointed to fill the vacancy. Mr. N., it was admitted on all hands, had been a most attentive faithful and honest keeper and left at his decease, a destitute family. The appointment of his widow, so far as I know, gave general satisfaction. Of one thing, I am certain, which is, that she has discharged the duties . . . in a most careful and faithful manner, and no charge of neglect or want of fidelity can be sustained against her. Having resided for forty years in the immediate vicinity, and in view of the Light, I can testify that it has never been in a better condition than since it has been under her charge, nor is there any Light upon the Coast, superior to it.[50]

Angeline Nickerson kept her appointment until 1859. Shown in the photo on previous page in the late 1850s, the towers were moved in the 1870s to escape erosion and were replaced with conical cast-iron towers in 1877. (Courtesy of the USCG Historian's Office)

## St. Marks Light Station (1842)

The flourishing cotton trade prompted the establishment of aids to navigation at Appalachee Bay, Florida. The first tower built at St. Marks River was found to have hollow walls, not the solid brick called for in the contract cosigned by Winslow Lewis. The second tower, completed at no cost to the government in 1830, soon displayed large cracks and a faulty foundation on an eroding sand bank. In 1842, Lewis was forced to tear the lighthouse down and rebuild it on a solid foundation of pilings. Heavily bombarded during the Civil War when used as a Confederate lookout and signal tower, the tower was repaired and a new lantern with a fourth-order lens installed in 1867. The tower height was increased 10 feet beneath the lantern in 1883. Shown here in 1893, the lighthouse remains the oldest active lighthouse on the Gulf of Mexico in 1999. (Herbert Bamber photo courtesy of the USCG Historian's Office)

## Gurnet (Plymouth) Light Station (1843)

Built in 1768, the first lighthouse at Gurnet Point, on the north side of the entrance to Plymouth Bay, Massachusetts, consisted of a 20-foot-long structure with a lantern at each end. The station survived a stray cannonball from a British ship aiming at a nearby fort during the Revolutionary War, but it succumbed to fire in 1801. Twin towers were built in 1803 so that mariners would not confuse this station with the single light at Barnstable. An inspector pointed out that they were too close together and at a short distance appeared as a single light. The towers were rebuilt in 1842, and, like their predecessors, were too close together. One tower was discontinued and removed in 1924; the other continues to function as an active aid to navigation in 1999. (National Archives #26-LG-7-11)

## Cape Poge Light Station (1844)

In addressing Massachusetts' Cape Poge Light in his 1843 report, Revenue Cutter Capt. Michael Connor stated,

> Cape Poge light stands on the last end of Martha's Vineyard, is an excellent light and well kept and I think indispensable in guiding vessels over the shoals from both directions. The Tower is wood having been built over forty years, and now in need of repairs. I think a new and substantial one, on the modern plan should be substituted here. This light also guides vessels to the Harbour of Edgartown, which is a resort for an immince [*sic*] number of vessels, and the Nantucket Whale Ships nearly all fit out from this place—in the fall and winter, the Harbor is spacious and admits vessels of the largest class, it is four miles from Cape Poge & has a class lighthouse on the end of a pier at the entrance of the Harbour . . .[51]

A 30-foot wooden octagonal tower on a rubblestone foundation was built in 1844. Additions were made to the 1801 dwelling in 1843 and 1869. (In the 1878 photo above, the 1843 addition is the section to the left of the chimney, with the original 1801 section to the right.) A fourth-order Fresnel lens was installed in 1857. Keeper Edward Worth is shown on the lantern gallery. He was first appointed in 1848 when the Whigs came into office; he lost his appointment soon after they lost power in 1853. Worth returned as keeper in 1866; his son, Jethro, was appointed his assistant in 1867 and replaced his father as principal keeper in 1882. In 1883, Jethro accepted an appointment at a less isolated station at the Harbor Light in Edgartown.[52]

The 1879 *Annual Report* stated that the sea had washed away all four acres purchased at Cape Poge in 1801 and nearly all of the additional four acres purchased in 1825. Part of the station was swept into the sea during a gale in 1892 and a new tower was authorized in 1893. The 1893 tower, erected 40 feet from the old one, used the old tower's lantern and lens. The old tower was dismantled; its foundation began its descent down the sea bank in 1896. Moved several times away from eroding cliffs, the 1893 tower survives in 1999. (Courtesy the USCG Historian's Office)

## Long Island Head Light Station (1844)

Also referred to as the Inner Harbor Light, the Long Island Head Light was established in 1819 at the north end of Long Island, Boston Bay, Massachusetts. The tower was rebuilt of iron in 1844, making it one of the first iron-plate towers constructed by the Lighthouse Service. In 1845, Keeper Charles Beck is reported to have run a signal system for pilots in Boston Harbor. He would hoist up a black ball to indicate when more pilots were needed to guide ships into the harbor. (National Archives #26-LG-7-35)

## West Chop Light Station (1846)

The West Chop Light Station on the west side of the entrance to Vineyard Haven Harbor on Martha's Vineyard off the Massachusetts coast was established in 1818. Because of encroaching seas, it was rebuilt in 1846 on a more protected site. The white tower of rubble masonry covered with shingles shown here was fitted with a fourth-order lens in 1857. A steam fog signal and a one-and-a-half-story frame dwelling, connected to the tower by a covered walkway, were added in 1882. In 1888 the dilapidated stone dwelling built in 1817 was torn down and a frame house built on its foundation.

In 1891 the masonry tower was in such poor condition that it was demolished and a new, taller tower built on its foundation. (Courtesy of the USCG Historian's Office)

# Little River Light Station (1847)

Located on Little River Island at the mouth of Little River, Maine, the Little River Light Station was established in 1847 to guide vessels into the refuge at Cutler Harbor. In 1850, Cutler had a population of 820; its local industries included fishing, shipbuilding, and manufacturing of herring boxes. In 1876 the fifth-order lens was moved from the tower shown here to a cast-iron cylindrical tower. (Courtesy of the USCG Historian's Office)

## Biloxi Light Station (1848)

The light at Biloxi, Mississippi, is the most prominent landmark on the Gulf Coast. The tower was prefabricated of cast iron (possibly the first in the South to be so constructed) with a balustrade encircling the watch room, and was brought by ship to its permanent location along the roadbed of the old Spanish Trail. Today the tower rests on a circular concrete base in the median of a major highway.

Women tended this light longer than any other light in the United States. Mary Reynolds was in charge from 1854 until 1866 (although the light was probably dark throughout the Civil War). She was succeeded by Perry Younghans, who died within the year. His widow Maria assumed his duties and continued at her post until 1919. She is remembered for having stayed at her post during several severe hurricanes, in spite of having her dwelling flooded. She was succeeded by her daughter Miranda, who remained until 1929. (National Archives #26-LG-34-22A)

# West Sister Island Light Station (1848)

West Sister Island Light was established in 1848 at the Maumee Bay entrance on the west end of Lake Erie, Ohio. According to the *Annual Report,* a new lens apparatus was installed in 1857 and the tower supplied with "an interior brick cylinder, cast-iron stairway, stone caps and sills, cast-iron deck-plate and lantern of modern design." The tower survives as an active aid to navigation in a National Wildlife Refuge. (National Archives #26-LG-48-13)

## South Pass Light Station (1848)

The first lighthouse at South Pass in the Mississippi Delta, Louisiana, was swept away in a violent storm, the second decayed in five years, and a third was built in 1848. The New Orleans collector requested at 60-foot iron tower, but the Fifth Auditor proposed another wooden tower. It was not until 1881 that South Pass received a 105-foot iron skeleton tower placed 100 feet south of the old rotting tower. (Courtesy of the USCG Historian's Office)

# Greenbury Point Shoal Light Station (1849)

Established in 1849 on the Severn River mouth at the north entrance to Annapolis Harbor, Maryland, the 35-foot tower reportedly had nine lamps and 14-inch reflectors in 1854. It was refitted with a sixth-order lens in 1855. The Light-House Board began recommending a new screwpile structure in 1878: "The land about Greenbury Point is washing away, and eventually the light-house will be in danger. The light, in its present position, is of little use, and is so small that it can hardly be distinguished from the lights of the Naval Academy and the harbor of Annapolis." A hexagonal screwpile lighthouse, no longer extant, replaced it in 1891. (National Archives #26-LG-22-24)

Acting upon the Secretary's suggestion, Pleasonton issued the following instructions.

## INSTRUCTIONS

## TO THE KEEPERS OF LIGHT HOUSES WITHIN THE UNITED STATES

1. You are to light the lamps every evening at sun-setting, and keep them continually burning, bright and clear, till sun-rising.

2. You are to be careful that the lamps, reflectors, and lanterns, are constantly kept clean, and in order; and particularly to be careful that no lamps, wood, or candles, be left burning any where as to endanger fire.

3. In order to maintain the greatest degree of light during the night, the wicks are to be trimmed every four hours, taking care that they are exactly even on the top.

4. You are to keep an exact amount of the quantity of oil received from time to time; the number of gallons, quarts, gills, &c., consumed each night; and deliver a copy of the same to the Superintendent every three months, ending 31 March, 30 June, 30 September, and 31 December, in each year; with an account of the quantity on hand at the time.

5. You are not to sell, or permit to be sold, any spirituous liquors on the premises of the United States; but will treat with civility and attention, such strangers as may visit the Light-house under your charge, and as may conduct themselves in an orderly manner.

6. You will receive no tube-glasses, wicks, or any other article which the contractors, Messr. Morgan & Co., at New Bedford, are bound to supply, which shall not be of suitable kind; and if the oil they supply, should, on trial, prove bad, you will immediately acquaint the Superintendent therewith, in order that he may exact from them a compliance with this contract.[60]

7. Should the contractors omit to supply the quantity of oil, wicks, tube-glasses, or other articles necessary to keep the lights in continual operation, you will give the Superintendent timely notice thereof, that he may inform the contractors and direct them to forward the requisite supplies.

8. You will not absent yourself from the Light-house at any time, without first obtaining the consent of the Superintendent, unless the occasion be so sudden and urgent as not to admit of an application to that officer; in which case, by leaving a suitable substitute, you may be absent for twenty-four hours.

9. All your communications intended for this office, must be transmitted through the Superintendent, through whom the proper answer will be returned.

Fifth Auditor and Acting Commissioner of the Revenue

TREASURY DEPARTMENT

FIFTH AUDITOR'S OFFICE
*April 23d,* 1835

# III. The U.S. Light-House Board Improves the System

When complaints about the poor quality of Winslow's system of lamps and reflectors continued to flow into Congress, another board was appointed in 1851 to scrutinize every aspect of the Lighthouse Establishment. The investigation found a myriad of problems. Some towers were not tall enough to provide the necessary range for their lights; their placement along the coast was erratic: they were bunched together in populated areas and scattered in sparsely settled areas. Mariners testified that they could not see or distinguish the lights, placing blame on the now-obsolete lamps and reflectors. The investigating board recommended that the whole system be revamped under the direction of a nine-member board. The U.S. Light-House Board, established by Congress in 1852, redivided the country into 12 districts, appointed an army or naval officer as inspector as well as an engineer in each district, issued rules and regulations for the overall management of the lighthouse system and detailed instructions to the individual keepers for operation of the lights, devised a classification of lighthouses, and mandated the use of the Fresnel lens. The Board raised the heights of many towers, lighted many dark sections of the coast, and issued an annual *Light List*, an expanded list of aids to navigation detailing the location and characteristics of every aid to navigation in service.[1]

The Light-House Board took advantage of evolving building technology to build more towers offshore, often replacing expensive lightships. Extensive and detailed drawings were prepared, leaving little to the imagination of the builders. "Plans of light-houses of different classes, with modifications adapted to different localities, would promote economy by the frequent repetition of the same pieces, which in stone-work, brick-work, iron-casting, carpenter's work, glazier's work, and the like, is productive always of a decided economy."[2] Less reliance was placed on the old contract system of hiring the lowest bidder to build lighthouses. "A knowledge of the qualities of stone, cements, mortars, and other materials used in their construction, is not to be acquired in a day, and belongs only as a general rule, to a competent engineer, architect, or builder."[3] Personnel from the U.S. Army Corps of Engineers were detailed to design and construct many of the lighthouses completed under the Light-House Board.

A regular system of inspection of the lighthouses was put into place. Because customs collectors acting as superintendents generally lacked the expertise to carry out this duty, a new position was created.

> Frequent visitation and minute examinations by competent inspectors would insure vigilance, economy, and order on the part of the keepers. The inspectors should be men thoroughly acquainted with all the details of light-house management and superintendency, with the manner of adjusting the lamps and reflectors, and of keeping them in order.[4]

The Light-House Board also addressed problems caused by leaky lanterns and towers, the smallness and heaviness of the lanterns, and poor ventilation within the lanterns; the lack storage space for oil and other supplies; the frequent necessity for repointing the towers; disconnected lightning rods; the lack of comforts in the keeper's dwellings; infrequence and hastiness in effecting repairs at the lighthouses; and ineffective notices of changes in the lights.[5]

Under the Board, each light was classified according to its position and use. Primary coast lights were located at the most prominent points along the coast. Secondary lights were located on the inferior points along the coast and in broad sounds and bays. Next were those on minor sounds and bays, and harbor and river lights. In the last classification were range, beacon, and pier lights.[6] The more important the classification, the larger the order of lens used. First-order lenses provided the largest range; sixth-order provided the smallest. In addition to expanding the information contained in the *Light Lists*, the Board developed a system of distinguishing characteristics involving different numbers of flashes at timed intervals, as well as use of color.

Screwpile lighthouses were introduced in the United States with the construction of the Brandywine Shoal Lighthouse in 1850. The design, which originated in England, was found most suitable for protected waters such as bays or sounds where the bottom surface was too soft to support a heavy tower. A lightweight wooden tower rested on iron legs, or columns, which were tipped with cork-screw-like flanges.[7]

*Thimble Shoals Lighthouse, Virginia (*Harper's New Monthly Magazine, *March 1874)*

Within a few decades, as many as 100 protected screwpile lighthouses were built throughout the United States, primarily in the Carolina Sounds and Chesapeake Bay, but also in the Gulf of Mexico. One screwpile built in the Great Lakes at Maumee Bay survived only a short time. This type of structure was suited to slow-moving, shallow water that was not subject to freezing; the principal enemies of this type of lighthouse were fast-flowing water, ice, and fire.

Sturdier screwpile or diskpile lighthouses for exposed sites were designed for use on the Florida coral reefs. They varied from the protected screwpile type in that the structure was a tall, skeletal iron tower as opposed to a squat wooden one. This made the light visible for much longer distances than was needed in the protected bays and sounds. Lenses were elevated higher and were also heavier; first-order lenses weighed a number of tons.[8] The second difference was in the screw flanges. Large, iron-foot plates or disks were added

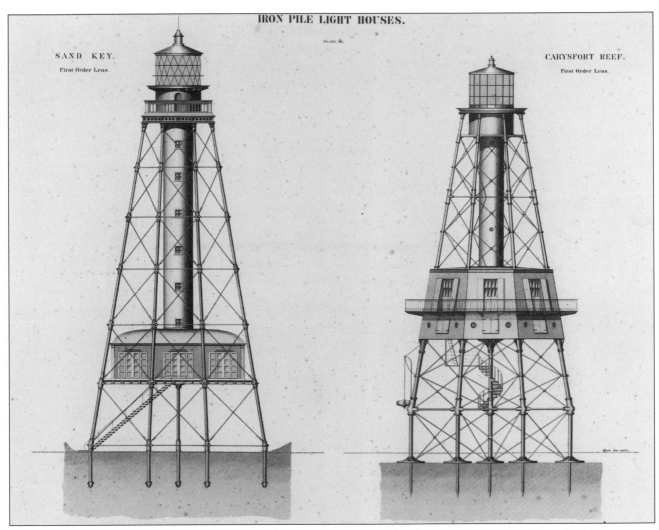

SAND KEY.
First Order Lens.

Scale ⅛.

CARYSFORT REEF.
First Order Lens.

*Architectural drawing of Carysfort Reef and Sand Key Light Stations, Florida, from National Archives, RG 26*

above the screw tip in order to diffuse the pressure caused by the weight of the tower. Six lighthouses of this type were constructed in the Florida reefs, three before the Civil War and three after. Those built before the war are much simpler in appearance than those built decades later.

The Light-House Board believed lights on prominent capes or points should "not be less than 150 feet above the mean sea-level, to enable the mariner to be warned of his danger in time to shape his course, with the least loss of time, for his destined port; or, in the event of bad weather, to haul off with comparative safety."[9] By 1859, nine brick towers over 150 feet tall had been built, and

six more were constructed after the Civil War; all were coastal lights of the first order. The tallest, Cape Hatteras Light in the Outer Banks of North Carolina, was 193 feet.[10] These tall towers were conical in shape, except at Cape Romain, South Carolina, which was six-sided. All but one of the 15 towers remain standing. All were built along the Atlantic Coast, the farthest north being Fire Island Light, New York, and the farthest south Dry Tortugas Light, Florida.[11]

Many masonry towers built on sandy soil first had piles driven into the ground. On the piles a cribbing consisting of several layers of 6- by 12-inch timbers was laid; on this were placed several courses of granite. At some sites, such as Cape Hatteras and Bodie Island, the sand was so compact that piles were not needed; after scraping away the loose upper layer of sand, the builders laid only the wood grillage and granite foundation.[12]

The United States Navy took possession of the California coast during the war with Mexico in the 1840s. The treaty of Guadalupe, which ended that war in 1848, officially ceded the territory to the U.S. government. The California coast had no aids to navigation until after gold was discovered there in 1848. The first prospectors arrived by ship after an 18,000-mile voyage around Cape Horn. The transcontinental railroads had not yet been built.[13] Eager prospectors streamed across the Rockies on horseback, in wagon or stagecoach, or on foot. Ships, however, were the most economical way of moving supplies and equipment; steamship lines were besieged with more passengers than they could carry. San Diego and San Francisco were the only good natural harbors on the California coast. Ship captains soon demanded lights and foghorns to steer vessels away from the rugged headlands, underwater ledges, rocky outcroppings, and treacherous islands. Merchants supported them with a petition sent to the Secretary of the Treasury in 1851:

> We the undersigned merchants of San Francisco beg leave respectfully to suggest to the Department the great and immediate necessity of establishing a Light House near the entrance of this Harbor—the want of one has caused great detention, inconvenience, as well as the total loss of many vessels bound to this port.[14]

Their demands were submitted to the newly constituted (1852) Light-House Board, which erected 16 lighthouses on the West Coast between 1852 and 1858, all designed by Ammi B. Young, an architect employed by the Treasury Department. The basic design for all 16 consisted of a simple cottage dwelling with a tower rising through the roof. The Baltimore firm of Gibbons and Kelly was contracted for their construction. The first one was built on Alcatraz Island in San Francisco Bay to guide the way to the city that was the center of the gold mania and to aid the ferries crisscrossing the Bay.

Tall towers were generally not required on the West Coast because lighthouses could be placed atop the cliffs and headlands that fringe the Pacific. In fact, care had to be taken not to locate them at too high an elevation, where their light could be obscured by the frequent fog, which made fog signals as vital as the lights. Structural styles soon ranged from small brick cottages (Battery Point, Point Pinos) to an elaborate Stick/Eastlake wooden combination tower/residence (Point Fermin, Mare Island). Most distinctive to California were squat, large-lens structures situated on the major headlands (Point Reyes, Cape Mendocino).

The 1848 act establishing the Territory of Oregon provided for two lighthouses. The Coast Survey was charged with recommending appropriate sites for these and other lighthouses to be placed on the West Coast.

## SIDEBAR: Fog Signals

The first fog signal used in the United States was a cannon installed at Boston Harbor Light Station in 1719. The Boston keeper would answer a shot from a ship entering the harbor, giving the mariner a sense of the direction of the lighthouse. The most common early fog signal was a bell rung by hand. Fog bells rung mechanically were introduced in the early 1850s. They were operated by a striking mechanism and weight that was raised by either a flywheel or clockwork. Many of these bells were located in a wooden pyramidal bell tower. In 1854 the bell buoy was introduced, followed by the whistling buoy in 1876.

*Drawing of Cape Elizabeth bell tower from National Archives, RG 26*

Celadon Daboll developed the compressed-air fog trumpet that was powered by hand or by a horse and tested it at Beavertail Light Station, Rhode Island, in 1851. Although the trumpet produced a more penetrating sound than the bell, the care required for the horse discouraged its widespread use. Steam-powered signals proved far more efficient; steam-powered whistles were introduced in the late 1850s. In 1866 the reed horn signal powered by a caloric engine was also introduced.[15]

Usually fog signals were added to existing light stations; at Manana Island, a fog signal station (pictured on next page) was developed not far from the Monhegan Light Station. In 1853 the Light-House Inspector in Portland, Maine, wrote the following:

> The island of Monhegan is the island that all our vessels on this coast take their
> departure from on leaving the coast . . . and is the only land that steamboats wish to
> make between Portland light and Whitehead light . . . before you change your course
> . . . The Manana is a small island, taken . . . out of Monhegan Island on the westerly side,
> and makes the harbor of Monhegan. . . . A sailing vessel is obliged to run until she

*Manana Island Fog Signal Station in Maine (top) and 1898 Patos Island fog signal building in Washington State housing a Daboll trumpet (bottom). (National Archives #26-LG-3-40 and #26-LG-62-32)*

judges herself up, and then lay to until the fog clears. Often a vessel or steamboat may be within a cable's length of this island in the fog, and not know whether they are near or not, or whether they lay inside or outside the island. A bell, well arranged on Manana, would announce to a vessel the position of the island. . . .[16]

In 1856 a fog bell, struck by machinery, was placed on Manana Island, about one mile west of Monhegan Island Light off the coast of Maine. A dwelling must have been built for the keeper, for the 1868 *Annual Report* states that it was repainted that year. In 1870 a 10-inch Daboll trumpet replaced the bell. In 1872 a steam fog-whistle replaced the trumpet, which was removed to Portland Head. In 1999, a diaphone horn is used. (National Archives #26-LG-3-40)

*1873 drawing illustrating the interior of a fog signal building for a siren. (National Archives, RG 26, Entry 6A)*

A siren fog signal was first installed at Sandy Hook East Beacon, New Jersey, in 1866. By 1890, fog signals in use included "sirens, trumpets, steam whistles, bell-boats, bell-buoys, whistling buoys, bells struck by machinery, cannons fired by powder or gun-cotton, rockets, and gongs."[17]

Construction of lighthouses slowed considerably during the Civil War; the hostilities played havoc with the lighthouse system. Immediately after secession, the Secretary of the Light-House Board, Commander Raphael Semmes, U.S.N., resigned his federal position to accept a post in the Confederate Navy. The Confederate States formed their own Lighthouse Bureau with Semmes as chief, but he had been in charge there only a week when the war broke out; he left to outfit and command the commerce raider CSS *Sumter*.

At the start of the war in April 1861, federal supply vessels and buoy tenders were armed "to protect them against lawless persons who might attempt to capture them or to interfere with their movements whilst performing their legitimate

*Mobile Point Lighthouse at Fort Morgan, Alabama, soon after its capture by Union forces in 1864. Note the temporary light structure to the left of the tower. (U.S. Naval Historical Center photo #NH 51942)*

duties."[18] Delivery of supplies was limited to north and east of the Delaware state line.

The towers in the Gulf states passed from Union to local control and were supported by state funds, with the exception of towers in the Florida Keys, which were held by Union forces throughout the war. These lighthouses required protection, however. An October 11, 1861, letter from the Secretary of the Treasury to Secretary of the Navy Gideon Welles indicated that

> A band of lawless persons have recently attacked the lighthouses and destroyed or removed the expensive illuminating apparatus from the two

important lights at Jupiter Inlet and Cape Florida, and the Department have been informed that the two important lights at Carysfort Reef and at Dry Bank, near Sombrero Key on the Florida reefs have been threatened.

Commander Pickering, lately the Light House inspector on that Coast, is of opinion, and in this opinion the Light-House Board fully concurs, that a small vessel properly armed and drawing not over seven feet water could protect all the lights on the Florida Reefs and do other efficient service by cruising in the South Channel between Cape Florida and Sombrero Key . . .[19]

The U.S. Light-House Board Improves the System

Many of the Confederate collectors in the Gulf states began to extinguish the aids along the coast in hopes that Union ships would founder on unlit shores. Most removable property was transported to safer locations. The tall towers served as excellent vantage points along the low Gulf coast to spy on blockader movements or advancing military troops. Of the four dozen towers in operation along the Gulf Coast, the two at Dry Tortugas operated under Union control throughout the war, eleven were relit by the end of 1862 and another seven by war's end. Most suffered from vandalism, fires, military exchanges, and/or neglect. Not until 1875 would the Gulf lighthouses stand in their prewar condition.[20]

With 164 lights discontinued, the Lighthouse Establishment did the best it could to relight, as combat conditions permitted, the major lights that had been extinguished; special buoys, lights, and lightships were placed to facilitate military operations. Many Union keepers at southern stations felt the need for protection not only from Confederate troops but often from their "secessionist" neighbors as well. The troops assigned to protect some stations provoked complaints from keepers who charged them with damaging and looting property they were assigned to protect. Progress in relighting and repairing the lights was hampered by the loss of district engineers and inspectors to military posts. Even so, most of the lights that had been discontinued were repaired and relit by 1866.[21]

# Sankaty Head Light Station (1850)

The first Fresnel lenses in the United States were installed in the Twin Towers at Navesink, New Jersey, in 1840. No others were installed until a special act of Congress directed that two other lighthouses be equipped with these superior lenses: Sankaty Head on Nantucket, Massachusetts, and Brandywine Shoal in Delaware. Two years after its completion in 1850, the Light-House Board investigations found Sankaty Head to be one of the most solidly constructed lighthouses in the country. The lamp for its second-order Fresnel lens burned only as much oil as "required for a small beacon light in any of our rivers and harbors, fitted with ten lamps and reflectors." This same tower continues as an active aid to navigation with its red stripe serving as a daymark. (Courtesy of the Society for the Preservation of New England Antiquities)

## Straitsmouth Island Light Station (1850)

A letter from keeper John Davis at Straitsmouth Island Light, dated April 7, 1843, described the lighthouse serving Rockport, Massachusetts, as

> a most miserable concern, Altho it has been built not quite eight years, yet it is neither wind nor water tight. While I am writing to you, there are icicles cleaving to the inside of the walls as thick as a man's wrist, and extending from the top to the bottom of the building. I do sincerely hope that the Department will authorize it to be rebuilt during the coming summer and located where it ought to be, i.e., 87 yards toward the sea from where it now stands. True, it would be rather harder for the

keepers, inasmuch as it would carry it that much further from the dwelling house; but that circumstance ought not to be thought of for a moment, when the property and lives of our seafaring brethren are in jeopardy. The N.E. part (point) of this Island, round which many hundreds of vessels yearly pass, is low, rocky and very dangerous; therefore the light ought to be located as far seaward as practicable.[22]

Seven years later, in 1850, the white octagonal tower shown on the previous page was completed. It was refitted for a Fresnel lens in 1857. According to the 1873 *Light List*, the plank walkway led over the rocks upland toward a one-story white dwelling. In 1896 a white cylindrical tower replaced the masonry tower. (National Archives #26-LG-9-57)

## Execution Rocks Light Station (1850)

Legend has it that in the days of Niew Amsterdam, the Indians used the shoal as an execution place for their white prisoners. The need for this light off the west end of Long Island Sound in New York was mentioned in an 1838 report by Lt. George M. Bache of the U.S. Navy. He thought that a lighthouse was preferable to a lightship because the lighthouse would accommodate a "more perfect lighting apparatus, and consequently, a more brilliant light . . ." The lighthouse would never change position as would a lightship, so vessels could "run for it with greater confidence." Bache added that, "being placed on the reef, it will be a better guide for both passages around the rocks than a light-vessel anchored near the shoal . . . it will prove more economical in a series of years." The report estimated that in 25 years, $102,500 would have been expended on the lighthouse but $115, 000 on the light-boat (a difference of $12,500 in favor of the tower), and that at that time it would be necessary to renew the boat while the tower would still be standing. Designed by Alexander Parris, the granite tower with brick lining was first lit with lamps and reflectors in 1850; a Fresnel lens replaced the lamps in 1856. In 1868 a new keeper's dwelling was erected on a protective pier, a new lantern was placed on the tower, and the fog bell was replaced with a steam-operated trumpet. The 1873 *Annual Report* indicated that the fog signal was in operation for 284 ½ hours during that year. The tower and dwelling survive as part of an active station. (National Archives #26-LG-11-53A)

THE U.S. LIGHT-HOUSE BOARD IMPROVES THE SYSTEM

# Grindel (Grindle) Point Light Station (1850)

Grindel Point, on the north side of the entrance to Gilkey's Harbor in Maine, was the location of a lighthouse established in 1850. The keeper's dwelling was brick, with a red tower on top, elevating the lantern to 28 feet. The lighthouse is shown here shortly after it was refitted with a fifth-order lens in 1856.

The 1875 *Annual Report* indicated that the station had so deteriorated that rebuilding was advisable. The brick keeper's dwelling was replaced with a frame building; a square brick tower was built for the light. What remained of the old dwelling was reroofed and used as a covered way between the dwelling and the tower, and as storage space for provisions, fuel, oil, and supplies of various kinds.

When the light was decommissioned in 1934, local citizens petitioned the Bureau of Lighthouses to give the station to the town, to be used as a memorial to local mariners.[23] (Courtesy of the USCG Historian's Office)

THE U.S. LIGHT-HOUSE BOARD IMPROVES THE SYSTEM

## Prospect Harbor Light Station (1850)

Completed in 1850, the Prospect Harbor Lighthouse, Maine, was discontinued in 1859 because the Board felt it "not of sufficient service to the general or local interests of navigation to justify its maintenance." Relighted with a new fifth-order lens in 1870, the 1850 tower continued in service until 1891, when it and the attached granite dwelling were replaced with a detached wood shingle tower and a wood frame dwelling on the old stone foundation. (Courtesy of the USCG Historian's Office)

# Brandywine Shoal Light Station (1850)

A lightship served Brandywine Shoal in Delaware Bay, Delaware, until a tower with a straightpile foundation was erected in its place in 1827. A lightship served again after the 1827 tower was destroyed in 1828, but it was replaced with the nation's first screwpile lighthouse in 1850. The 1850 tower on a screwpile foundation was designed and constructed by two well-known engineers, Major Hartman Bache and Lt. George G. Meade, under the jurisdiction of the Bureau of Topographical Engineers. Using the Englishman Alexander Mitchell's screwpile design, they rectified the problem that had caused the collapse of the Minots Ledge Light that same year by cross-bracing the piles and surrounding the structure with a pile-supported fence and a second fence of riprap around the base to protect the tower from ice floes. On April 23, 1851, Col. I. I. Abert, Bureau of Topographical Engineers, reported:

> The brilliancy of the light by common report, far exceeds any of those in its immediate neighborhood. It is always seen when the state of the atmosphere permits, in a range which includes the lights on both the Capes, and those of Mispillion, Mahons Ditch, the Ledge and Egg Island.
>
> The goodness and sufficiency of the work has been amply tested by the storms of the past winter . . . That a work of so novel a description, erected at so exposed a point, should from the first be free from slight defects, require no changes, and exhibit no deficiencies, was more than those most sanguine in its ultimate success looked forward to.[24]

In July 1851, the light station was turned over to the Treasury Department with a complete inventory of all its contents, which included:

> three mechanical lamps;
> weights for the clock movement of the lamps;
> three cords "in use";
> three pulley rollers;
> one spare cord;
> a dustpan and variety of brushes;
> 12 tin rings to secure wicks;
> four tin dripping pans;
> one graduating tin cup;
> 13 iron chimneys;
> 105 glass chimneys;
> three tin lanterns;
> one signal lantern;
> one tin heater;
> 110 small sized wicks;

10 pieces of wick for tin table lamps;

98 round wicks for table lamps;

three oil tanks;

one tin pump;

one tin lamp feeder for table lamp;

one tin oil filler;

one stone water pitcher;

two pair of iron moulds;

two small pieces of calf skin;

one paper box containing 225 leather salves for lamps;

56 leather collars for burners;

one spirit level;

two iron rods for leveling lamps;

one tin box containing 12 ratstail brushes, 11 bone-handled brushes, 2 small cold chisels, 4 drills, punches for cutting leather, and 2 balls red roughe *[sic]*;

one demijohn, 1 ½ gallons alcohol;

one tin box containing 2 coils large-size wick, nails, one small stone, one iron stamp to press leather for pumps of lamps, and one wood stamp to press leather for pumps of lamp.

The 500-pound fog bell required a clock mechanism, a handle for winding, a roller, a rawhide rope, a wrench, and 300-pound weights. In addition to furniture, tools, and other household items, the station included two water barrels, a boat, and a blackboard for "noting operation of lamps."[25]

Shown on page 93 in 1891, the station was replaced in 1914 with a tower on a caisson foundation. (National Archives #26-LG-18-37)

## Whitehead Light Station (1852)

In 1803 Congress appropriated money to buy ten acres for a light station on Whitehead Island at the entrance to Penobscot Bay in Maine. Letters of accusation went to the Secretary of the Treasury stating that one of the very early keepers, Ellis Dowlf, sold oil supplied by the government for the lamps to private individuals. One stated that

> the Rev. Em. Hall informed me that he bought 2 gallons of oil of Mr. Dowlf measured in the lighthouse to him. David Linahen also told me that he bought 4 gallons measured as aforesaid . . . From the best information I can obtain, Mr. Dowlf has sold more than two hundred gallons of states Oil within two years.[26]

Whitehead has an association with many types of fog signals. In 1839, Andrew Morse installed a perpetual fog bell that was driven by a "boom" floating on the surface, which, as it rose and fell on the swells, caused the 2,000-pound weights to be wound up. Although unsuccessful because of its tendency to be broken up in the surf, it served as a precursor to the clockwork mechanism that was powered by a descending weight.[27] Maintaining these new fog signals required special skills of the keepers. A letter from Josiah Sturgis, a Captain in the U.S. Revenue Service, reported that Mr. Morse complained that

> the keeper of the light and Bell at Whitehead, Mr. Bartlett, is a man who has been notorious for his dissipated habits, . . . and is entirely unqualified for doing anything with the bell machinery, justice to myself as this is an experiment as well as to government demands that the keeper should be a man of some mechanical skill, that he may be able to discover and correct any screw, nut, or pin that may be liable to work loose, and in season to prevent any further trouble that may result, the machine has suffered much for the want of such attention . . .[28]

In later years the Light-House Board appointed assistant keepers or machinists to specifically attend the fog signals at stations where it was warranted.

In 1852, a 41-foot conical tower was constructed on Whitehead, and a Jones fog bell hung in the scaffold. The fog bell mechanism malfunctioned

and was repaired two years later. In 1855 a third-order lens replaced the reflectors in the tower. A steam-powered fog signal was installed in 1869 and an extra cistern dug to increase the very limited water supply. In 1883 the lamps at Whitehead were switched from lard oil to mineral oil (kerosene), as were lamps at many other stations. In 1888 a brick building was constructed to hold the fog-signal machinery, cistern, and boilers. The water supply fell dangerously low in 1889, necessitating the use of sea water in the boilers for several months.

The keepers in this period (1875-1889) were Abbie Burgess and Isaac Grant. Abbie became famous at age 14 for keeping the light on Matinicus Rock during a long, stormy winter month when her father could not get back from Matinicus Island. She subsequently married the son of the keeper who replaced her father on Matinicus Rock, and both had official appointments as keepers at Whitehead until they retired in 1889.

In 1891 the old rubblestone dwelling shown here was demolished and replaced on the same foundation by a frame double dwelling. Whitehead is still an active aid to navigation. Its Fresnel lens is in the collection of Shore Village Museum in Rockland, Maine. (National Archives #26-LG-4-37)

## Dog Island Light Station (1852)

In 1838 a light station was established in Florida on the east side of the middle entrance to St. George's Sound. Dog Island is seven miles long and encompasses 2,000 acres. An early keeper, Jacob Myers, commented on the frequent storms, explaining in an 1839 letter to Stephen Pleasonton the "necessity of having a Sea going Sail Boat, being on an Island 25 miles . . . from Town. And exposed so much to an open and heavy sea, and all inclement seasons . . . and in the case of a Gale of Wind, or an over Flow, as did this Island experience September 1837, when one of the Pilots saved his life by hanging on to a tree . . ."[29] Keeper Myers also requested that an assistant keeper be appointed to his station so that he would not have to extinguish the light while going to town for provisions. Many stations along the Gulf of Mexico were able to justify the appointment of assistant keepers because of their isolated locations. We do not know if Keeper Myers's entreaties produced results; however, the records show that the turbulent weather continued. The 40-foot tower with a revolving light was damaged in an 1842 gale and replaced with a new frame tower in 1843. It, in turn, was blown down by a gale in the autumn of 1851 and replaced the following year by the whitewashed brick tower shown opposite.

The keeper's dwelling, built in 1855, was burned by the Confederates, and the lantern was used for target practice. The light was reestablished in 1866 after the station was again rebuilt. The new white dwelling stood on five iron screwpiles painted black.

Severe erosion over the next few years undermined the tower until it was a foot out of perpendicular. In 1872 the lens and lantern were removed from the tower and placed on top of the keeper's dwelling. Both the old brick tower and the keeper's dwelling were swept away by a hurricane in 1873. The station was never reestablished. (Courtesy of the USCG Historian's Office)

---

# Bull Bay Light Station (1852)

The 1839 *Light List* indicates that a lantern with eight lamps existed atop the keeper's dwelling at Bull Bay Light. The 1858 *Light List*, however, places the Bull Bay Light (established in 1852) at the north end of Bull's Island at the mouth of the Santee River in South Carolina (25 miles northeast of Charleston). A short tower stood on the brick keeper's dwelling. In 1856 the lantern was refitted with a fourth-order lens.[30] During the Civil War (1862) the lantern and lens were destroyed. The station was reestablished in 1868 with a new lantern and apparatus.

By 1886 erosion was undermining the dwelling. An earthquake in 1887 seriously cracked the walls and threw the lens out of position. Repairs were made. A brick oil house was built in 1892 to accommodate new mineral oil (kerosene) lamps. The station was seriously undermined by the sea in 1897 and discontinued in favor of a new site on Jacks Creek, to which everything that could be salvaged was moved. The new station was lit in 1900. (1893 image on page 98 by Herbert Bamber, National Archives #26-LG-26-18)

Bull Bay Light Station

---

## Hog Island Light Station (1852)

Hog Island Light was built in 1852 to guide mariners into Great Machipongo Inlet on the Virginia coast. The Civil War brought unique challenges to southern lighthouse keepers. Those keepers who sympathized with the Union often found themselves guarding their federal property and fearing neighbors sympathetic to the Confederacy. Some asked for protection by Union troops, later finding that this type of protection was sometimes worse than none at all. Such was the case with Jean Potts at Hog Island Light. On September 30, 1863, he wrote to the Light-House Board:

> I take the liberty to communicate to you the state of Affairs concerning the threats to destroy this Light House and also my life. On the 6th of August last I received information that the Light-House on Smiths-Island had been destroyed and robbed by 9 men, and that they had threatened

to commit this same outrage upon the Light-House of this Island and also take <u>me</u> [*sic*], dead or alive.

I could not obtain military aid from the main shore, as all the troups had left the County. My life was at stake as well as the public property, which I was determined to defend at all hazards. I kept watch (telescope in hand) from up the Light-House, for four hours, when I saw the Steamboat "Star" approaching the Matchopongo Inlet with troops on

board. I was confident then, that Aid was coming. Lieutenant Howk with 20 men of the 3th Pa. Artillery landed on the beach and reported himself as Commander of a Guard to protect the Light-House, which relieved me of my anxiety. Said Guard remained here for three weeks, when they were recalled to Fortress Monroe to join the Regiment, much for my relief; there were a set of armed ruffians amongst them, who stole everything where they laid their hands on and destroyed most every thing in their reach, instead to protect it. They even laid their hands on the public property, burned and destroyed great many shingles, filled some canteens with oil, stole a coat and a pair of pants, paint brushes, beeswax, shoepegs, emptied the Spr'ts of wine can, stole a pair of scissors, fishing lines, cut and took the sheetrope from the L.H. Boat, and made almost a wreck of her. They broke up nearly all my stools, crippled my Geese and robbed my henhouse. They also took the corn and vegetables out of the gardens and lots belonging to the poor citizens on the Island.

They stole a fine little fishing schiff from Samuel Kelly and many more things too numerous to mention, and had it not been for the better part of the men, God only knows the amount of Damage those ruffians would have done . . .

The slanderous attacks from the rebels and rebel sympathizers are getting up to such a pitch against me . . . I consider my life and honour . . . in peril . . . I have been repeatedly assailed and wronged by a set of reckless politicians and their creatures during this most treacherous rebellion. I have suffered enough here in this hornetsnest of Rebeldom and know too well that my unconditional Union principles have caused a bitterness against me among the rebels, which will lead to my destruction if they get a chance at me. If I was known among them as a coward they would have despatched [*sic*] me long ago.[31]

The 1852 tower shown on page 99 survived the Civil War but was replaced with a cast-iron skeletal tower in 1896. This tower was demolished in the late 1940s. (Courtesy of the USCG Historian's Office)

## Black Rock Range Light Station (1853)

At the south entrance to the Niagara River near Buffalo, New York, a set of range lights were completed and lit in 1853. The pier light, a rubblestone tower, was surmounted by a parapet of brick masonry which lofted a lantern containing a fifth-order lens. According to the 1870 *Annual Report*, "This beacon-light having been established to serve a temporary purpose, until the completion and exhibition of the light on Horseshoe Reef, and being of no use, will be extinguished at the close of navigation this season, and will not be relighted next spring." (National Archives #26-LG-43-23)

THE U.S. LIGHT-HOUSE BOARD IMPROVES THE SYSTEM

## Pumpkin Island Light Station (1854)

The light station built in 1843 on the northwest side of Pumpkin Island was located south of Buck's Harbor on Isle au Haut Bay, Maine. The white brick tower was connected by a workroom to a one-and-a-half-story keeper's dwelling painted brown. A fog bell was rung by hand in response to signals from ships. This photo, taken before 1880 when the dwelling was painted white, shows a lightning rod, a fire-prevention feature, on the side of the tower. (Courtesy of the USCG Historian's Office)

# Alcatraz Island Light Station (1854)

The first lighthouse constructed on the West Coast was on Alcatraz Island, strategically located just inside the entrance to San Francisco Bay. Its California cottage design, a dwelling surrounding a short cylindrical tower, became a prototype for several West Coast lights—Point Loma, Santa Barbara, Point Conception, Point Pinos, Fort Point, and Crescent City. It put the keeper's bedroom close to the lantern, so that only one keeper was needed.

The third-order lens at Alcatraz was lit in 1854. A fog bell, rung by hand, was added in 1856—essential in a bay where the fog rolled in off the Pacific nearly every day. Alcatraz Island was fortified in 1858 and became a prison for Indians and soldiers. Guards in the prison watch towers informed the keeper of approaching fog. A clockwork mechanism, wound every four hours, was later installed to strike the bell. By the turn of the century the keeper had three assistants to rotate the four-hour nightly watches.

Alcatraz became a maximum-security prison in 1909, its additions overshadowing the small lighthouse. The 1854 cottage was replaced with a much taller reinforced concrete tower, built just outside the prison in 1909. (National Archives #26-LG-63-2)

# Cedar Keys (Seahorse Key) Light Station (1854)

In surveying potential sites for lighthouses in Florida, Captain Richard Evans of the U.S. Revenue Cutter *Campbell* wrote in 1851:

> Seashore Key, the south one of a group called Cedar Keys, appears to have been formed by nature as a site for a Light House, having a high bluff on its southern extremity about 30 feet above the level of the sea, from which a shoal extends southwest fifteen miles and deep sandings close to it, thereby rendering approach in the night dangerous. I understand that the Cedar Keys have considerable commerce, being the depot for cotton brought down the Suwanee River amtg. to over 3000 bales per ann., and on the increase. I would therefore recommend a Light House on said Key, and would add that in my opinion the Lantern should be 100 ft. above the level of the sea.[32]

The small, square lighthouse with the light lantern in the center of its roof was designed by Lt. George Meade of the Topographical Corps of the U.S.

THE U.S. LIGHT-HOUSE BOARD IMPROVES THE SYSTEM

Army and built on this high hill in 1854. The building rested on granite pilings, had solid wooden shutters to protect the windows, and seated a fourth-order Fresnel lens in the lantern.

Federal troops occupied the island in 1861 and used the lighthouse as a prison. In 1896 a severe hurricane and tidal wave damaged Cedar Keys, decreasing its commercial importance. The light was extinguished in 1915; the station is now in a national wildlife refuge and is used as a marine laboratory by the University of Florida.[33] (National Archives #26-LG-31-27)

## East Pascagoula River Light Station (1854)

The Pascagoula River penetrates far into the rich pine forests bordering the northern shore of the Mississippi Sound. As the river enters the Sound, it forms a marshy delta that is confusing to navigate. The very modest one-and-a-half-story lighthouse shown above was built on the Mississippi coast in 1854. The tower at one end displayed a fifth-order lens. The 1855 *Annual Report* stated that "5 reflector lamps would probably be required to give a light equal to that of the single lamp in the 5th-order lens. The saving of oil effected by the use of these lens lights seems to be about 50 per cent."

The light was badly damaged by a gale in 1860. The following year the light was extinguished for the duration of the Civil War; in fact, it was not renovated and reexhibited until 1868. In the interim it was used as a smallpox hospital.[34] Rock and ballast were placed in front of the station several times during the following decades to protect it from erosion.

Dredging of the river mouth in 1888 led to the establishment of range lights the following year to aid navigation of the very narrow river channel. In 1906 the station was destroyed by a hurricane.[35] (Courtesy of the USCG Historian's Office.)

---

## Boon Island Light Station (1855)

The lighthouse on Boon Island guides a large fleet of fishing vessels in and out of York Harbor, the only safe harbor in a long stretch of Maine coast. Coastal steamers plying between Boston and Bangor, Portland, and St. Johns navigate according to the Boon Island Light. The rocky outcropping is six miles offshore and surrounded by dangerous ledges. The first tower on the island was built during the War of 1812. That tower was destroyed and rebuilt in 1831. It was replaced in 1855 by the tower shown opposite.

Boon Island is bare rock, with no soil for growing things, and was completely cut off from the mainland in stormy weather. The only communication was by boat (a telephone connection was not installed until 1902), but long periods of winter storms often made it impossible to launch a boat. The keepers and their families sometimes ran very low on food and supplies, and worried about starvation. On one occasion a distress signal flown from the lighthouse caused a passing schooner to drop a barrel of food overboard, timing it so that it washed into the single cove on the island where the keepers could reach it.[36]

Living conditions were not very comfortable, either. The keeper's dwelling contained two sets of quarters, forcing the second assistant keeper to board with one of the other families. Conditions were so cramped that vegetables and provisions were stored in the halls. "While the interior walls of the [keeper's] dwelling were of good coursed, quarry-faced, granite masonry, it had long leaked badly from defective linings and a defective roof, and was cold and unsuitable for occupation by families at that exposed and isolated station. Its entire interior was therefore torn out, wholly rearranged and rebuilt, and a framed upper story added."[37] A third dwelling was not built until 1905.

THE U.S. LIGHT-HOUSE BOARD IMPROVES THE SYSTEM

Lard oil lamps were used at Boon Island until 1883, when much cleaner mineral oil (kerosene) was introduced. The onerous task of ringing the fog bell by hand was one of the keepers' duties until after the turn of the century. (National Archives #26-LG-1-40)

## Monomoy Point Light Station (1855)

Monomoy Point Light is on the southern extremity of Cape Cod, marking sand shoals that extend eight miles south from the town of Chatham, Massachusetts. A lighthouse was first built there is 1823 to serve the extensive local fishing fleet. Severe weather damaged the tower, and it was replaced in 1855. The new tower was of cast-iron-plate construction, painted red, with a white lantern topped by a black dome. A covered walkway connected the tower with the one-and-one-half-story white keeper's dwelling. In 1857 the tower was lined with brick and a fourth-order lens was installed in the lantern. The braces shown here were later replaced with guy wires that ran from the gallery to the foundation; they kept the tower from swaying in high winds.

By 1872 the light was considered insufficient to guide the oceangoing traffic that depended on it. The recommended larger lens was never installed, however, and in 1923 it was decided that Chatham Light was sufficient for the area. Monomoy Point Station was sold and used during

THE U.S. LIGHT-HOUSE BOARD IMPROVES THE SYSTEM

World War II as a practice bombing range.[38] After the war it became a National Wildlife Refuge administered by the Fish and Wildlife Service. The station was restored in 1988 and is used as an educational center by the Cape Cod Museum of Natural History. (National Archives #26-LG-8-51)

## Bristol Ferry Light Station (1855)

Bristol Ferry Light in Rhode Island is on a strait between two islands in Narragansett Bay—water that is impossible to navigate at night without a light. In 1846 a private steamer company placed a lightship there and asked the federal government to replace it with a light on Bristol Neck. In response, a small brick keeper's house was constructed in 1855 with an attached square tower 28 feet tall, housing a sixth-order lens. Twenty-five years later a copper-ribbon lightning rod was added to protect the lantern during storms. Deactivated in 1927, the station is now a private residence. (1884 photo, National Archives #26-LG-11-23)

# Seven Foot Knoll Light Station (1855)

This one-story iron screwpile lighthouse was built on the Chesapeake Bay at the mouth of the Patapso River near Baltimore, Maryland, in 1855. Circular in shape, 40 feet in diameter, built of cast-iron plates, it rested on nine iron legs, cross-braced and also tied to the center pole.[39] A fourth-order lens sat in the lantern; a fog signal was struck by machinery. In 1884 ice damaged one of the iron piles. Wood piles secured by cables were placed around the lighthouse in bunches of 10 (15 bunches in all) as a temporary barrier to ice. In 1894 a fuel platform was built under the superstructure. The clusters of oak piles were disintegrating at that time, as is evident in this photo, so heavy riprap was deposited all around the lighthouse to protect it from future ice. More riprap was added in 1897 and in 1903.

In 1987 the Seven Foot Knoll Lighthouse was moved ashore to Pier 5 in Baltimore's Inner Harbor. (1885 photo by Major Jared A. Smith courtesy of The Mariners' Museum, Newport News, Virginia)

## Petit Manan Light Station (1855)

Built in Maine in 1855, the 119-foot Petit Manan Light tower pictured above replaced an earlier 53-foot tower, built in 1817, which had a lantern too small to light the rugged Maine coast. The new lantern housed a second-order Fresnel lens. A fog bell hung in the scaffold to the left. By 1868 the bell had cracked and was replaced. The following year 18 of the cast-iron steps up the tower were damaged when the weights of the machinery that revolved the lens fell. Both were repaired.

The steam engine that ran the fog signal was supplied with fresh water by a well dug in the rock. Because most of the water drained from a nearby swamp, it was polluted by vegetable matter that gummed up the boiler. In 1870 a cistern was dug to provide more fresh water. Five years later two wooden tanks were placed in the cellar of the former keeper's dwelling, and two water sheds were erected at each end of the building, fitted with water conductors and gutters to catch additional rain water. The following year another large brick cistern was added under the water shed, doubling the water supply.

By 1887 the watch room and lantern had been loosened by vibration in high winds, and were secured by an iron collar and a set of iron tie rods. Thus the lantern survived the fierce gale of December 1887.

A protracted period of dense fog and little rain in the spring and summer of 1889 exhausted the water supply so that sea water had to be used in the boilers for several weeks. Cistern capacity was again increased.

In 1899 the characteristics of the station changed when cellars were excavated in the rock, dwellings moved to the new locations, an old stone dwelling demolished, and the rain shed extended 30 feet. In 1999 the station continues as an active aid to navigation in a National Wildlife Refuge. (Courtesy of the USCG Historian's Office.)

---

## Port Pontchartrain Light Station (1855)

New Orleans was built on an Indian portage in Louisiana between the Mississippi River and Lake Pontchartrain, a hundred miles upstream from the Gulf of Mexico. With currents in the river too swift for sailing ships, the easiest route for early commerce was through the interior lake, 42 miles long and 26 miles broad. After the introduction of steamboats (1811), lighthouses were established at several locations along the route. Two canals and a railroad (built in the 1830s) connected Lake Pontchartrain to New Orleans, simplifying commerce and attracting summer vacationers.

An 1835 letter from the Port Pontchartrain Rail Road Company to the New Orleans collector urging the federal government to replace their private light describes the great improvements and changes that had already taken place:

> since the harbor has opened for business, an almost total change has taken place in the intercourse and trade between all places from whence the approach to the City is via the Lakes,—that the business is now carried on by regular trading Steam Boats—that the number of persons who have passed this year is ten times greater than was ever known before the Harbor was made—that there are now twelve regular trading Steamboats making from two to three trips per week and at least eight others intended for the trade which will increase the number to twenty in the course of nine months. . . .[40]

In 1854 Congress appropriated money to replace the 1839 wooden tower at Port Pontchartrain with this substantial brick tower, designed by Captain Danville Leadbetter to sit on the mucky lake bottom at Port Pontchartrain. Its base was a concrete pad atop pilings.[41] During the Civil War keeper Charles Fagot was the only keeper who stayed at his post when the Confederate government took over southern lighthouses. The image below shows the tower before 1880, when the top of the brick tower was flared out to accommodate a larger lantern.

For the last 48 years of its service, the keepers at Port Pontchartrain were women: Ellen Wilson from 1882 to 1895; Margaret R. Norvell, appointed in 1896 after Ellen Wilson's death; and Mrs. W. E. Coteron, who replaced Mrs. Norvell in 1924, serving until 1929.[42] (Courtesy of the USCG Historian's Office.)

## West Rigolets Light Station (1855)

Pictured here is the West Rigolets Light, located close to Fort Pike in Louisiana, completed in 1855 on the bayou that is Lake Pontchartrain's outlet to Mississippi Sound. After Fort Pike was occupied by Union troops in 1862 and the light station reactivated, keeper Thomas Harrison was shot during his second night on the job—the only keeper known to be killed at his post during that conflict. His murderer was never identified. Hurricanes did frequent damage, but the lighthouse was in operation until 1945. (National Archives #26-LG-39-42)

## Point Pinos Light Station (1855)

During the planning for building a light station on Point Pinos, the Superintendent of the U.S. Coast Survey in Washington received a box containing three cubes of stone from the quarry near Monterey. The sender wrote that "the two pieces of limestone are from the lower quarry: as you see it is very soft, but it is said to harden by exposure to the atmosphere. Cotton Hall at Monterey—quite a large structure, is built of it, and seems to answer the purpose very well. There are several other buildings of this stone, some of them of many years standing (as for

THE U.S. LIGHT-HOUSE BOARD IMPROVES THE SYSTEM

instance the old church of Guadalupe, erected 1794) and still in good condition."[43] The Coast Survey of 1851 listed three sites from which to obtain the stone to be used in the building.[44]

The first keeper at the cottage-style light station on Point Pinos was a veteran ordnance sergeant named Charles Layton. Within a year he was killed while serving in a posse chasing a notorious outlaw. His penniless widow, Charlotte, with four sons and a daughter to support, badly needed his appointment, and she received it in 1857. The gold rush interested most men more than lighthouse keeping, and Charlotte earned $1,000 a year, a substantial sum in those days; her assistant was paid $800. When she married her assistant, she stepped down to let him become head keeper.[45] (Courtesy of the USCG Historian's Office)

Point Pinos Light Station

# Farallon Island Light Station (1855)

The Farallon Islands lie 30 miles offshore from San Francisco, California. Rocky and treeless, often rising steeply out of the sea, they provide few easy landings for small boats and were a dire hazard for large ships. Indeed, the Spanish name of the islands means "rock rising from the sea."[46] One island in the South Farallon group is three-quarters of a mile long, three-fifths of a mile wide, with a peak 340 feet high. It was once populated only by sea birds.

Russians came from Alaska after 1810 to harvest sea otter pelts.[47] During the 1850s gold rush prospectors came from the mainland in nesting season to collect eggs for sale in San Francisco, an activity that led to immense rivalry and some open combat among collectors and keepers. In May 1881 a U.S. Marshal and 21 soldiers solved the problem by evicting all non-government personnel from the island.[48]

A light station was established there in 1853, but the first tower was built for lamps with reflectors rather than for the huge first-order Fresnel lens that arrived in 1854. The tower had to be rebuilt in 1855 to accommodate

THE U.S. LIGHT-HOUSE BOARD IMPROVES THE SYSTEM

it.[49] Finding keepers at the $500 salary authorized by Congress was difficult, because domestic servants in San Francisco could earn more than that during the gold rush. The first keeper was a stockholder in an egg company who was more interested in his dividend than in the light.[50]

The early keepers made fish and rabbits a large part of their diet. They hauled soil from the mainland to make gardens, and they raised pigs, goats, and chickens. They kept a donkey or mule to pull cargo up a little railroad that connected the landing with the keepers' houses and to haul five-gallon cans of oil on a pack saddle up the hill for the lamp every day.[51]

The lighthouse was built of stone, with an iron tower holding a first-order lens.

> [The lens] has eight sides, each made up of concentric prisms above a bulls eye in the center. There are 33 prisms about the bulls eyes, and the glass of the thickest is about six inches through. The whole lantern revolves about the lamp by clockwork once in eight minutes. . . . The Lamp has five concentric wicks, and is fed by an elaborate contrivance to keep a continuous and copious supply of oil for each wick.[52]

Four keepers kept watch through the night to make sure the lamps were burning. In foggy weather the siren also had to be monitored. ". . . The keepers have to do all the repairing and some new construction—for they have a forge, a lathe, and full set of machinists' and carpenters' tools."[53] A tender came with supplies and mail every three months if the weather was calm enough for a landing. Often it was not.

A unique fog signal developed by Major Hartman Bache was used at this station from 1859 to 1871, when a severe storm destroyed it. A locomotive whistle was mounted in a brick chimney over a natural blowhole in the rocks. It worked splendidly in windy weather, but unfortunately, foggy days were often calm, with insufficient wave action to force air through the whistle. Nor did it work at low tide. It was replaced by a steam siren in 1879.[54]

One of the most isolated light stations in the country, Farallon Island took a toll on its keepers. Three families did not always get along well, and there were charges of inattention to duty, thievery, and drunkenness. An entire staff was dismissed for selling oil for their own profit. Children died of illness before help could be obtained, and keepers died in rescue attempts when ships ran aground on the islands.[55]

The keepers' dwelling was razed in 1969, and the station automated in 1972. The light station is now located in a bird refuge. The first-order lens is at the San Francisco Maritime Museum.[56] (Drawings and photo courtesy of the USCG Historian's Office)

THE U.S. LIGHT-HOUSE BOARD IMPROVES THE SYSTEM

## Franklin Island Light Station (1855)

A light station was established in 1805 on Franklin Island near the mouth of St. George River in Maine's Muscongus Bay. The 1839 *Light List* recorded that it had 10 lamps with 14-inch reflectors, and stood 50 feet above the high watermark.

In 1853 the lighthouse inspector wrote that "the tower [is] entirely worthless, and lantern worn out, and the keeper's dwelling so old and leaky that [it is] unhealthy."[57] The Franklin Island Light was rebuilt in 1855, with a fourth-order lens on a white tower, 54 feet above sea level. The 1873 *Light List* described it as a brick tower, whitewashed, connected by a brick workroom to a one-and-a-half-story dwelling, painted brown. This photo was taken before 1879, when the *Annual Report* stated that the dwelling had been painted white. A fog bell was rung by hand. The tower remains today as an active aid to navigation, but without the dwelling. (National Archives #26-LG-2-24)

# Gay Head Light Station (1856)

Gay Head Lighthouse on Martha's Vineyard, Massachusetts, was established in 1799 to mark the south entrance to Vineyard Sound and the point vessels would run for when coming from sea and Long Island Sound. Rebuilt as a first-order light in 1856, the revolving lens contained 72 panels with 1,008 prisms.

As the photos below and on the facing page indicate, Gay Head became a popular destination for sightseers. Since lighthouses were often the focus of popular curiosity, the 1881 Instructions to keepers provided some guidance on hospitality. Keepers were directed to be "courteous and polite to all visitors . . . and show them everything of interest about the station at such times as it will not interfere with their light-house duties." Keepers were cautioned not to allow visitors to handle the apparatus or scratch their names on the lantern glass or tower windows. Nor were keepers allowed to charge for the privilege of touring the property.

(Late 1880s photos by Baldwin Coolidge courtesy of the Society for the Preservation of New England Antiquities)

The U.S. Light-House Board Improves the System

# St. Croix River Light Station (1856)

Ship captains wanted a light on Dochet Island (also called Big Island) at the entrance to the St. Croix River in Maine. The master of the steamer *Pequasset* wrote the local collector of customs in 1853 that

> the 'Big Island,' ten miles below Calais, is another point difficult to pass in the night; in fact, it is never attempted by heavy vessels, being directly in the center of the river, with numerous ledges and small islands on the American side of it. . . . Sixty vessels, ranging from 500 to 1,300 tons, have been loaded at the ledge this season, and, but for the great drought, the number would have been nearly double. Over 1,500 vessels, exclusive of steamboats, . . . have arrived and sailed from that port last year.[58]

The dwelling—a one-and-a-half-story white house—was erected in 1856, with a light tower on the south end. A fifth-order lens was placed in the lantern in 1869. The fog bell was struck by hand in answer to signals from ship captains. This station burned in 1976, with only the oil house extant. (Courtesy of the USCG Historian's Office)

THE U.S. LIGHT-HOUSE BOARD IMPROVES THE SYSTEM

# Narrows Light Station (1856)

This screwpile light, constructed in 1856, lit the entrance to the Narrows in Boston Harbor, Massachusetts. By 1863 a vessel had run into and damaged the structure. In 1867 severe winter weather carried away the ice breaker built around the structure to protect it. It was rebuilt "of oak piles secured by girders ballasted with stone, planked all over, shod with iron, and painted with red lead." Similar repairs were needed in 1882. The station was destroyed by fire in 1929. (National Archives #26-LG-8-65A)

Narrows Light Station

# Black River Light Station (1856)

The Black River Light Station was established in 1836 at the mouth of the Black River where it empties into Lake Erie in Ohio. Located 30 miles west of Cleveland Light, 50 miles east of Sandusky Light, it was to serve as both a harbor and a lake coast aid to navigation. A beacon was placed at the end of the west pier at the harbor's mouth. The 1838 *Annual Report* noted that "At three different times last year, such was the violence of the waves that persons endeavoring to light the beacon were washed from the pier, one of whom drowned."

Black River Light Station

THE U.S. LIGHT-HOUSE BOARD IMPROVES THE SYSTEM

The earlier tower was rebuilt in 1856. The 1868 *Annual Report* noted that "the tower, which was built of brick of inferior quality, is cracked, owing to the action of waves on the crib work" beneath it. It was repaired the following year and an elevated walkway built to "enable the keeper to reach the light in bad weather."[59] The tower is no longer extant. (National Archives #26-LG-43-22)

---

## Browns Head Light Station (1857)

In 1832 a 20-foot light tower was built of rubblestone and lime mortar on the northwest end of Vinalhaven Island at the entrance to Fox Island Thoroughfare off the coast of Maine. The tower apparently weathered badly, and was replaced in 1857 by the brick tower shown here, 39 feet above sea level attached to the one-and-a-half-story wooden keeper's dwelling, painted brown. A fifth-order lens replaced the reflectors in the earlier tower. The dwelling is today the residence of the town manager, while the tower is an active aid to navigation. (Courtesy of the USCG Historian's Office)

# Matinicus Rock Light Station (1857)

On a small island barely a half mile long, 20 miles off the coast of Maine, towers first of wood, then of stone, were undermined by wind and wave. The towers pictured here were built in 1857 of granite blocks, carefully hewn, with the courses tightly bound together, and connected to the keepers' houses by covered passageways.

In 1853, before these towers were built, Samuel Burgess received the keeper's appointment and took his wife and five children to this isolated station. His 16-year-old daughter Abbie earned lasting fame in 1856 by keeping the lights burning for an entire month when stormy weather prevented her father from returning from Matinicus Island five miles away.[60] As the wind and waves rose higher and higher, flooding their dwelling, she moved her mother and sister into one of the towers, even rescuing her chickens between waves. A year later Abbie performed with similar fortitude when her father was kept away for three weeks by vicious weather.[61] She must have watched the building of the really solid towers that stand today with much appreciation. (Courtesy of the USCG Historian's Office.)

THE U.S. LIGHT-HOUSE BOARD IMPROVES THE SYSTEM

## Cape Flattery Light Station (1857)

Cape Flattery on tiny 18-acre Tatoosh Island lies at the entrance to the Strait of Juan de Fuca in Washington State, the most northwesterly point in the continental United States. The lighthouse shown here was completed in 1857 in spite of "the Indian hostilities in Washington and Oregon Territories and the difficulties attending operations at such distant and sparsely populated localities. . . ."[62] In 1863 the Acting Collector of the Puget Sound District wrote as follows:

> On the first day of the current fiscal quarter two assistant keepers at Tatoosh (Cape Flattery) Light—Messes. Noyes and Moore resigned their positions on account of apprehended danger on the Island for want of a small boat. The only boat on the rock had been swept away during a violent storm last winter and the Light-House Board had been unable to replace it.[63]

The cottage from which the unusually tall tower (65 feet) lofting a first-order lens rises proved to be unusually damp (rainfall averages 100 inches a year) and was used as a work room rather than a dwelling from 1875 until 1894. In the above 1898 photo four keepers (two holding babies) and three wives stand in front of their double frame dwelling (erected in 1875). A steam-powered fog signal (installed in 1871) used the chimneys of the building to the right of the lighthouse. It required a large fuel house, a cistern holding 33,000 gallons, and a watershed of 3,000 square feet. A boathouse erected in 1877 was carried away by a tidal wave the following year and was rebuilt on higher ground. (Ca. 1890s photo by Herbert Bamber, National Archives #26-LG-61-4)

In 1883 "A pump was placed in each of the two kitchens and connected with the cistern, 130 feet from the dwelling, as it . . . often happened during the stormy season that for several days at a time it was almost impossible to carry a pail of water from the cistern to the house."[64] A well was dug in 1887 to supplement the water supply. In 1894 crowding in the frame keeper's dwelling led to the rehabilitation of the cottage so a keeper could use it. In 1897 a new brick fog-signal building was erected and a 15,000-gallon water tank placed on a brick foundation on the south side of the main dwelling.

In an 1898 feature article a visitor to Cape Flattery wrote that the only

> means of regular communication with the outside world is the canoe of the Indian mail-carrier. He makes the seventeen-mile trip from Neah bay (weather permitting) twice a week and also transports passengers to and fro for a consideration . . . [One] veteran carrier has had three canoes smashed to kindling wood at various times in endeavoring to make a landing through the surf. Often the only way to get the mail ashore is to throw it from the bobbing canoe to a rock, where the keeper stands ready to catch it.[65]

Cape Flattery Light is still an active aid to navigation.

---

# Seguin Island Light Station (1857)

The light station on Seguin Island, the first in Maine on an island,[66] was perched high on a hill just north of the mouth of the Kennebec River in 1795.  It was among the first constructed by the federal government. The wood tower blew down in 1819, and was replaced by a stone tower in 1820.[67] A fog bell was installed in 1837. A letter from Stephen Pleasonton to the Secretary of the Treasury in the 1830s described the island:

> Seguin Island situated 6 miles from the mainland. The lighthouse, with the dwelling is located 300 feet above the sea. The ascent of the road from the landing is an angle of 45 degrees, up which all the supplies have to be conveyed. The island contains about 50 acres of rocky land. No wood and very little land fit for cultivation, but produces sufficient grass to support several cows and a few sheep.[68]

A fog signal was installed in 1854, and the keeper's salary increased $100 annually for attending to the fog bell.

The white cylindrical granite tower shown in the photos on page 131 was rebuilt in 1857 to hold a first-order lens—the first Fresnel lens installed in Maine.[69] A short enclosed passageway connected the tower to the new, one-and-a-half-story brick dwelling. The frame building beside the tower was built in 1880 for the storage of fuel for a steam fog signal installed in 1873. Drought in Maine in 1890 led to the use of sea water in the fog signal boilers and necessitated the building of a reservoir to collect fresh water. A tramway was built in 1895 from the boat landing to the dwelling and is the only one still operating in the state of Maine. (Top photo on page 131 taken by Henry Peabody in the late 1880s, courtesy of the Society for the Preservation of New England Antiquities; bottom photo of boat landing courtesy of the USCG Historian's Office)

## Dutch Island Light Station (1857)

A light station that guided ships into Dutch Island Harbor and through the west entrance of Narragansett Bay was established in 1826 on the south end of Dutch Island near Jamestown, Rhode Island. Lt. George M. Bache's report of 1838 indicated that the lighting apparatus was faulty: the lamps were not firmly secured in their places and were moved up and down as the oil supply diminished; this changed the angle of the reflectors and made them almost useless.[70]

It appears that a second story was added in 1857 to elevate the tower an additional 16 feet. The replacement lantern with its fourth-order lens is shown here atop a two-story square brick Greek Revival dwelling. The fog bell on the side of the tower, operated by machinery, was added in 1878.

Dutch Island was automated in 1947. The following year the keeper's dwelling was demolished. In 1979 the detached tower was deactivated and turned over to the State of Rhode Island to become part of Bay Islands State Park. (Courtesy of the USCG Historian's Office)

## Marshall Point Light Station (1857)

A light station was established in 1831 at Marshall Point near Port Clyde on the coast of Maine. In 1839 Keeper William Perry queried Secretary of the Treasury Woodbury as to whether there would be any objection to him teaching six hours each day in a small district school situated close to the lighthouse. The local collector saw no objection as long as it did not interfere with his lighthouse duties.[71]

By 1855 the old rubblestone and lime mortar tower had weathered to the point that it needed to be replaced. The tower shown here was completed and lit in 1857. By 1880 the old stone dwelling needed extensive repairs. In 1889 the covered walkway was re-anchored to six stone piers. In 1891 the barn and fuel house were rebuilt, the latter connected to the dwelling by cutting a door through a wall. A boathouse was built in 1892. The old stone dwelling was struck and badly damaged by lightning in 1895. The following year the stone house shown here was demolished and replaced by a wooden dwelling on the same foundation. In 1898 a fog signal tower was built, a bell struck by machinery installed, and a telephone connection established with the hotel at Port Clyde village.

The walkway is no longer covered, but the station is an active aid to navigation and a popular museum. (National Archives #26-LG-3-47)

# Deer Island Thorofare Light Station (1858)

The Deer Island Thorofare Light (known locally as the Mark Island Light) is located on Mark Island, not far from Stonington, Maine. Built in 1857 and first lit in 1858, the square brick tower, whitewashed, was attached to a one-and-a-half-story wooden dwelling, painted brown. The 1898 *Light List* mentions a fog bell tower and a red brick oilhouse. The station is still an active aid to navigation. (Courtesy of the USCG Historian's Office)

Erie Land (Presque Isle) Light Station

THE U.S. LIGHT-HOUSE BOARD IMPROVES THE SYSTEM

## Erie Land (Presque Isle) Light Station (1858)

Established in 1818, the original lighthouse at Erie, Pennsylvania, was among the first light stations erected on the Great Lakes.

> The harbor of Erie is the largest and best found on Lake Erie, being between four and five miles long and about one mile wide, affording sufficient room to accommodate any amount of shipping. The neck of land that joins Presque Isle to the main has been wearing away for some years, and unless arrested, will destroy this valuable harbor . . . The harbor . . . is much resorted to by shipping of the lake, for shelter; and unless the island which forms it is protected from being washed away, the general government will . . . lose one of its finest harbors . . .[72]

Because the older tower was sinking, a new brick lighthouse (shown opposite) was constructed to hold a third-order Fresnel lens in 1858. Writing on this photo indicates that this tower served Presque Isle Light Station from 1858-1867. An unstable foundation apparently required another replacement tower, this one constructed of Berea sandstone. Serving until 1880, the 1867 tower was sold at public auction in 1881, "with the exception of the lantern, illuminating apparatus, iron stairs, and other parts which could be of further use to the Establishment, which were stored in the depot at Buffalo."[73] It was repurchased, restored, and relighted in 1885, and was discontinued in 1899. (National Archives #26-LG-46-79)

## Sombrero Key Light Station (1858)

For Sombrero Key, Lighthouse Engineer Capt. George Meade considered building a masonry structure or an iron structure on a masonry foundation before opting for the less-expensive iron diskpile structure like that already built at Carysfort and Sand Key reefs. Meade asked for an additional appropriation to cover the cost of galvanizing all the metal to protect it from exposure to the sea. Meade's estimate to complete the project came to $118,405.60; however, the final cost was $153,158.81—more than anticipated but less than a masonry structure. Preliminary work was interrupted by a severe hurricane in 1856; construction began again in 1857 and was completed in 1858. The first keeper, Joseph Bethel, maintained a home in Key West for his wife and five children. The Florida reef stations each had three keepers (one principal and two assistants) so that one was always on duty; they could not accommodate the keepers' families.[74] (Drawing on page 138 from Standard Plans, National Archives, RG 26; photo on page 139, National Archives #26-LG-33-34A)

IRON PILE LIGHT HOUSE.

First Order Lens.

DRY BANKS OFF COFFIN'S PATCHES.

Scale &.

Mean low water

Focal Plane 140 f.º above mean low water

Sombrero Key Light Station

THE U.S. LIGHT-HOUSE BOARD IMPROVES THE SYSTEM

# West Quoddy Head Light Station (1858)

Located inshore of a dangerous ledge of rocks on the Bay of Fundy near Lubec, Maine, West Quoddy Head Light was the easternmost light station in the United States. President Thomas Jefferson ordered its establishment in 1808 to guide burgeoning coastal shipping along a rockbound coast. The brick tower shown here was rebuilt in 1858 and displayed a third-order lens 133 feet above sea level.[75] Its red-and-white horizontal stripes made it a distinctive daymark as well as a nighttime beacon for navigators. The one-and-a-half-story dwelling, painted white, was connected to the tower by a brick workroom.

This coast regularly experiences treacherous fog. "The first fog warning device was a 5-foot cannon fired in response to the whistle of a nearby ship." In 1820 it was replaced by a 500-pound bell, struck by hand, a task compensated by an additional $70 for the keeper, who earned $250 annually.[76] Eventually a 10-inch steam-whistle fog signal was housed in a white brick fog-signal house (shown at right in photo below). (1892 photo courtesy of the USCG Historian's Office) The station is still intact in a state park.

THE U.S. LIGHT-HOUSE BOARD IMPROVES THE SYSTEM

## Wood Island Light Station (1858)

The original Wood Island Light Station on the east side of Wood Island near the Saco River entrance on the Maine coast was established in 1808 and guided ships to Winter Harbor. In the *Annual Report* of 1857, the Light-House Board boasted that "at the close of the fiscal year ending June 30, 1858, there will be in this district no lights fitted with expensive and inefficient reflectors and lamps of the old system."

The whitewashed stone tower shown here was constructed in 1858 to house a fourth-order lens. The frame dwelling was originally connected to the tower and workroom by a wooden walk, but at some point after 1873 the walk was covered against inclement weather. The fog bell tower, "with Steven's striking apparatus and a cast-steel bell weighing 1,315 pounds,"[77] was added in 1873. In 1890 "a 1,200-pound bell of bell-metal was hung, to replace the old steel bell, which was badly eroded."[78] The station survives as an active aid to navigation in a bird sanctuary. (Courtesy of the USCG Historian's Office)

# Willapa Bay (Cape Shoalwater) Light Station (1858)

The light at Willapa Bay on Cape Shoalwater was established in Washington Territory in 1858, one of 16 original lights on the West Coast.[79] It was built in the cottage style popular then. Construction materials and supplies were landed with the help of local Native Americans and their canoes.

Drifting sand was a continuing problem. A bulkhead was sunk around the lighthouse in 1868 to keep sand in place. The following year the keeper was told to plant shrubs in the sand around the bulkhead in a further effort to stop the drifting. Fences were put up in 1875 for the same purpose. In 1876 a board fence enclosed 25 acres for pasturage, which suggests that the keepers kept livestock. In 1879 a 400-foot plank road was built to aid in moving supplies over the sand drifts. The old boathouse, destroyed the previous year in a storm, was replaced by a new one located nearer the lighthouse and but 100 feet from the adjacent lifesaving station. Mineral oil lamps were installed in 1880. Willow trees and brush fences were tried

THE U.S. LIGHT-HOUSE BOARD IMPROVES THE SYSTEM

as sand barriers in 1881. More were planted the following year and the pasture fence, buried in sand, was taken up and moved back 200 feet. Two thousand square feet of the yard around the lighthouse were planked (as shown above in ca. 1890s photo by Herbert Bamber, National Archives #26-LG-62-2). In 1886 the plank road between the lighthouse and the barn was completely rebuilt and raised 2 to 3 feet above ground. The boathouse was moved 150 feet nearer the water and free from sand drift. In 1888 the boathouse and part of the fencing were blown away. In 1892 brush mats were placed around the bulkhead that enclosed the dwelling. The photo opposite shows the station in 1898. (Photo by Herbert Bamber, National Archives #26-LG-62-3)

Undermined by erosion, the 1858 lighthouse at Willapa Bay was deactivated in 1940 and later replaced with a modern tower.

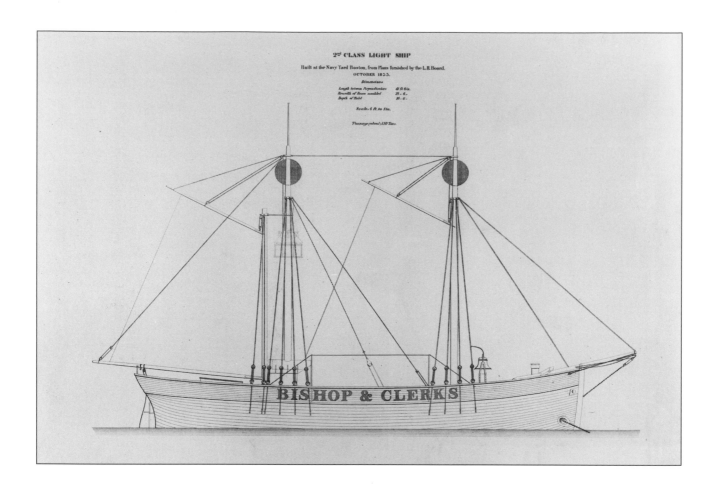

## Bishop and Clerks Light Station (1858)

In 1855 a lightship was placed to mark the hazard known as the Bishops and Clerks in Vineyard Sound off the Massachusetts coast. (Architect's drawing from Standard Plans, National Archives, RG 26 )

A lighthouse was built and lit on the rocky ledge in 1858, with a fifth-order lens in the lantern. The lead-colored tower attached to the side of the light tower in 1869 held a fog bell struck by machinery every 15 seconds.[80] A large quantity of riprap was placed around the base in 1889 to protect the foundation from erosion. (Photo opposite courtesy of the USCG Historian's Office)

In 1923 the lighting apparatus was changed from oil to acetylene, the fog bell discontinued, and the station automated. In 1952 the structure was determined to be unsound and was demolished. It was replaced by a 30-foot, white, pyramidal, slatted-wood day beacon.

# Windmill Point and Point aux Roches Light Stations (1858)

The first lighthouse built on Lake Champlain was Juniper Island, completed in 1826. It replaced a private beacon established by one of the many shipping companies that plied the length of the lake. In 1858 the Light-House Board constructed three lighthouses using a similar design. Pictured here are Windmill Point Light Station at the northern end of the lake in Vermont and Point aux Roches Light Station on the New York side north of Plattsburg. Both towers used dark blue limestone; however, the attached house at Windmill Point is granite and the one at Point aux Roches is wood. Note that the lantern panes in each are trapezoidal. The decline of lakeborne commerce contributed to the demise of active light stations on the lake.[81] Both stations survive but under private ownership. (Windmill Point photo opposite, National Archives #26-LG-17-53; Point aux Roches photo below courtesy of the USCG Historian's Office)

Windmill Point Light Station

THE U.S. LIGHT-HOUSE BOARD IMPROVES THE SYSTEM

Point Aux Roches Light Station

## Michigan City Light Station (1858)

The first keeper of the new light (an 1837 structure was replaced in 1858) at Michigan City, Indiana, was a Mr. Clarkson. He was followed in 1861 by Miss Harriet Colfax, who may have received a political appointment through a congressman cousin. She was 37 and was paid $350 a year. Critics of the political influence that won her the appointment mentioned her petite size and seeming fragility, but Colfax performed her duties without fail for 43 years, retiring in 1904 at age 80 because of failing health.

In 1871 an elevated walkway and beacon light were located on the 1,500-foot east pier guarding the entrance to Michigan City harbor. Harriet had to carry a lamp containing warm oil along the walkway to the beacon in every kind of weather. Her log entries frequently mention being nearly swept into the lake by waves crashing over the pier. In 1874 the beacon was moved to the west pier, 500 feet longer, which required the keeper to cross the creek by boat, walk along the other side of the creek, ascend the elevated walkway, climb the beacon ladder, and place the light. The elevated walkway was damaged so frequently that at times Colfax resorted to hiring a tug to get to the beacon.[82] (National Archives #26-LG-56-30)

# Pensacola Light Station (1859)

The first light station on Florida's Gulf Coast was established shortly after the United States acquired Florida from Spain (1821). A federal naval depot was constructed at Pensacola, the deepest port on the northern Gulf of Mexico. A lightship was briefly stationed there in 1823 while a naval base was being established, but rough seas kept it from anchoring in a

visible spot.[83] In 1825 an 45-foot tower was erected on a 40-foot sand bluff[84] on St. Rosa Island at the south side of the entrance to Pensacola Bay. In 1828, Keeper Jeremiah Ingraham reported, "The summer oil on hand is good, I have received no winter oil. The whiting is not good. The lantern is not fit for use. The oil butts are good but want painting. The window glass for the Light House is not fit to put in."[85] In 1839, Keeper Ingraham reported:

> This light house has now been in constant use for fourteen years, and is much out of repair. The clockwork is almost entirely worn out, so much so that it requires a very great additional weight to keep it running. The lamps too, are much worn, and should be replaced with new ones. The woodwork about the building is also become dilapidated and rotten, so much so, that the window frames are falling out.[86]

The Commandant of the Pensacola Navy Yard wrote the Collector of the Port on October 23, 1853, that "The lighthouse is thought to be well located, but altogether too low, as it is, from many points at sea, concealed by the lofty pines which abound on the coast."[87] To better serve the ships entering the port, the first tower was replaced in 1859 with the much taller conical brick tower shown here. A first-order lens operated 191 feet above sea level[88] until the Civil War, when gun battles put it out of operation. The first-order lens was probably sent to New York by the U.S. Navy.[89] Union forces relit the tower in 1862 with a temporary fourth-order lens. In 1869 the Light-House Board reinstalled another first-order lens and built a new dwelling for the keepers.

Lightning strikes in 1874 and 1875 necessitated installation of a new lightning rod. The 1878 *Annual Report* stated that "The tower is cracked inside beneath the lantern. During the rebellion this tower was struck many times by solid shot, and it is possible that some of the hurricanes since that time are beginning to make the effects of those shots visible and may have affected the stability of the tower itself." The tower was renovated in 1879 and stands proudly today, the grounds open to the public in the Pensacola Naval Air Station. (National Archives #26-LG-37-32B)

## Bergen Point Light Station (1859)

A light station was established in 1850 at Bergen Point on the New Jersey shore at the entrance to Newark Bay. In 1855 a sixth-order lens was installed, but the "crib on which [the dwelling] stands was originally built in the slightest manner possible, and without being entirely filled in. [It is] now decayed, or worm-eaten, and settling inwards, and the whole fabrics are in such a state as to be liable to be swept away by a heavy pressure of ice at any moment."[90] In 1857 a substantial stone pier was constructed for the foundation of a new lighthouse, shown above, which was completed in 1859. (National Archives #26-LG-11-19) The gray granite tower stands in the southeast angle of the wooden dwelling. A fog bell was struck by hand. In 1867 a cast-iron deck-plate was laid under the lantern, covering the stone deck of the tower. In 1873 the hand bell was replaced by a large bell struck by machinery.

In 1948 the superstructure of the Bergen Point Lighthouse was dismantled and replaced with a skeletal tower.

# Round Island Light Station (1859)

The light station on Round Island, Mississippi, in the Mississippi Sound off the East Pascagoula River, was established in 1833. The 1854 *Annual Report* described it as "badly built originally and now liable to be undermined by a heavy storm." The following year the keeper's dwelling was "old, not in good order, and is also being encroached by the sea."

The brick tower shown here and a detached, square keeper's dwelling with a verandah were erected in 1859, on a more suitable site northwest of the earlier tower. During an 1860 gale "keeper S. Fischer, with his wife and six children, huddled in the top of the tower as waves rolled across the island. For two days they awaited rescue without food or water. All they owned was lost. Every building on the island except the tower completely vanished."[91] Extensive repairs were needed.

"The Confederate States inspector at Mobile removed the [fifth-order] lens early in the Civil War and stored it at Montgomery. The island became a terminal for blockade runners and a haven for northern refugees during the war."[92] The light was relit in 1865. The tin roof on the two-story dwelling was replaced by shingles in 1879; an oil house was added for storing volatile mineral oil (kerosene) in 1891. In 1894 a 300-foot wharf was constructed. The station was deactivated in 1944. In 1954 a fire damaged the keeper's dwelling.[93] Title to the property was turned over to the City of Pascagoula in 1985; the tower was toppled in Hurricane Georges in 1998; however, there are plans to rebuild it. (Ca. 1890s photo by Herbert Bamber, National Archives #26-LG-37-60)

## Vermilion Pier Light Station (1859)

A compass lamp with a 14-inch reflector existed in 1849 on the west pier at the entrance to Vermilion Harbor on Lake Erie in Ohio.[94] The light was "renewed" and the pier repaired in 1852. Shown here after being repaired in 1859, the wooden tower held a sixth-order lens. The tower was damaged by waves in 1868; in 1872 a keeper's dwelling was purchased in the village. In 1878 the decaying wooden tower was replaced with a new one of iron erected on an oak foundation on top of the old crib work, which no longer exists. (National Archives #26-LG-48-9)

# Minots Ledge Light Station (1860)

Minots Ledge is named for George Minot, who lost a valuable, cargo-laden ship on the dangerous offshore rocks near the entrance to Boston Harbor, Massachusetts, in 1750. More than 40 vessels suffered the same fate

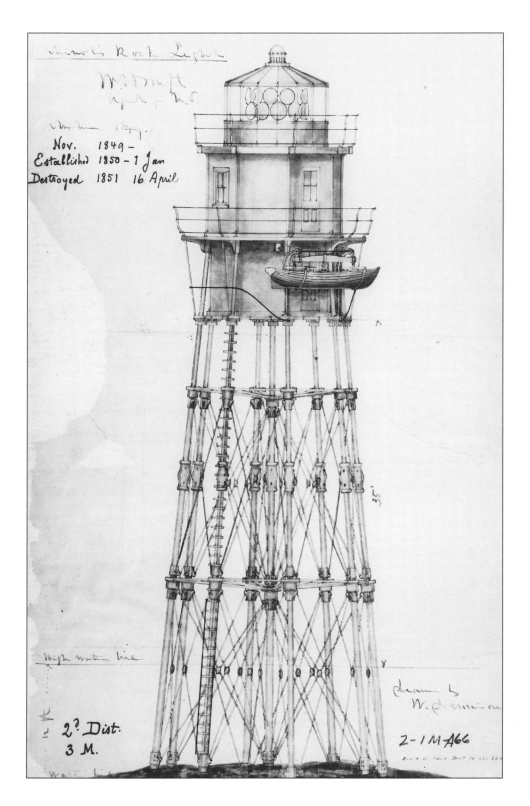

between 1832 and 1840. "There is hardly a winter passes that we don't have to record some fatal accident on or near Minots Rocks, owing to the want of a Light House."[95] The obvious need for a light on the ledge was met in 1850 with a tower built on an iron straightpile. (1847 drawing on page 155 from National Archives, RG 26) In March 1850 the keeper on Minots Ledge, Moses Dunham, appealed for an increase in salary, stating that his position was "arduous and trying, requiring the constant attention of himself and two assistants both by night and day. This lighthouse is . . . exposed to the force of the ocean sea in Easterly gales, . . . the vibration of the whole structure is great . . ." He stated that he would not stay beyond October if his present $600 per annum was not increased to $1,500. Secretary Pleasonton replied that he regretted losing such an experienced keeper, but he could not raise his salary above what other keepers were earning. Dunham and his assistants also wrote to their Congressman: "The sea would strike the piles 30 feet above the rock, solid water and with <u>tremendous</u> [*sic*] force & it seemed to me that every sea would brake [*sic*] it from the rock."[96] In 1851 a gale snapped the iron piles and swept this structure away, drowning two assistant keepers.

A lightship marked the ledge for the next nine years while a new masonry tower was being constructed. A remarkable engineering feat, the 1860 tower was designed by Joseph G. Totten based on British waveswept towers such as Eddystone. Work could proceed only between April and September at low tide on calm days. On days when landing was

The U.S. Light-House Board Improves the System

Minots Ledge Light
Station

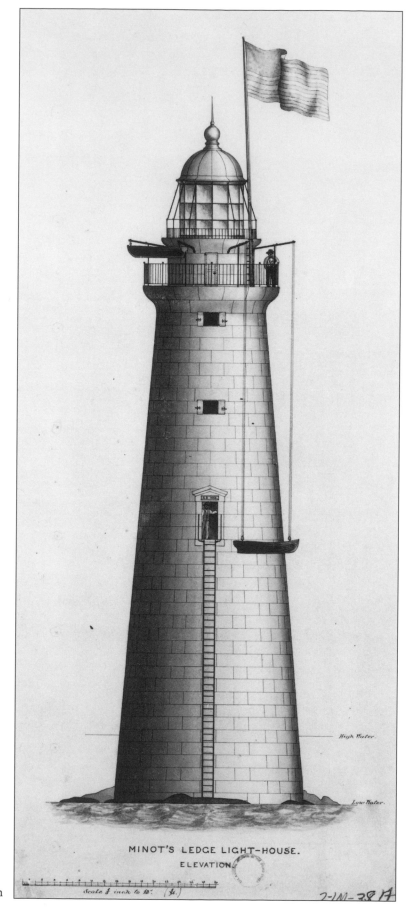

MINOT'S LEDGE LIGHT-HOUSE.
ELEVATION.

Scale ⅛ inch to 1¹²: (⅟₆.)

Minots Ledge Light Station

THE U.S. LIGHT-HOUSE BOARD IMPROVES THE SYSTEM

impossible, the workmen were engaged in cutting and fitting the interlocking granite blocks on nearby Golf (Government) Island, near Cohasset. The ledge itself took three years to prepare. An iron scaffolding 20 feet high was erected and strung with lines for the workmen to hold onto when waves broke over the rock. (National Archives #26-LG-8-24 on page 156) A boat with a lifeguard on board stood by at all times to pick up men washed from the rock. Temporary cofferdams were constructed from sand bags so the foundation stones, which lay more than two feet below high tide, could be cemented to the rock ledge. After much experimenting, mortar was spread on muslin cloth and wrapped around each stone before it was lowered into place. The mortar oozed through the cloth to form a good adhesion with the stone. A derrick, dismantled every day, was used to lay the courses of stone. The tower base was solid rock up to the level of the entrance door. (National Archives #26-LG-8-28 on page 157) The interlocking stones formed a monolith of great weight, which, combined with its conical shape, diverted the energy of the waves away from the tower, enabling it to withstand the heavy pounding of the surf.

The tower is cylindrical, 14 feet in diameter. (Drawing on facing page from National Archives, RG 26) Four iron floors divide the upper tower into five stories, where the keepers worked and stowed supplies. The keeper's dwelling was onshore in Cohasset. Minots Ledge Light Station was automated in 1947 and is still an active aid to navigation and an American Society of Civil Engineering Landmark.

## Isle of Shoals (White Island) Light Station (1860)

Established in 1821 at the boundary between Maine and New Hampshire, the old tower was described by Winslow Lewis in 1842 as "a conical rubble-stone tower . . . cased with wood outside to protect the masonry . . ." The early station also had a covered bridge leading to the tower. An 1841 storm destroyed this bridge as well as blew down the wood house and reportedly the keeper "was even obliged to take his Cow into his dwelling house."[97] In 1844, disgruntled former keeper Joseph Cheever wrote Stephen Pleasonton that his replacement "[is] so very lame, that he can seldom, if ever, go in the Lantern himself, and the person he has with him to take the charge of the Establishment, works for his rum and tobacco, and whose brains are nearly destroyed by the use of alcohol."[98] Mr. Cheever had hopes of being reinstated when the Whigs returned to power. The brick tower shown here with a second-order lens was completed in 1860. (Society for the Preservation of New England Antiquities photo by Henry Peabody, ca. late 1880s)

# Cuttyhunk Light Station (1860)

The Cuttyhunk Light, established in 1823, was on Cuttyhunk Island on the Massachusetts Coast near New Bedford. It guided mariners to both Buzzards Bay and Vineyard Sound. The original rubblestone tower and dwelling were so badly built that the tower was twice encased in brick, yet continued to leak. A fifth-order lens was installed in 1857. In 1860 the old tower was torn down, a second story placed on the keeper's dwelling, and the lantern placed as shown here.

By 1881 the dwelling was dilapidated and required renovation. In 1892 the old dwelling was demolished and replaced by new structures. The last keeper served until 1947, when the Coast Guard demolished the station. (Courtesy of the USCG Historian's Office)

# Admiralty Head Light Station (1860)

The first lighthouse to guide ships from the Strait of Juan de Fuca into Puget Sound was built on Admiralty Head on Whitby Island, Washington, in 1860. Its lantern atop the wood dwelling contained a fourth-order lens. A cistern was added in 1868. In 1875 space in the attic was enclosed and used as a watch room. A winch to move supplies up from the shore was added in 1880, and the station was fenced to keep out loose cattle grazing nearby. In 1882 the launching of boats from the boathouse was facilitated by a wooden tramway. A galvanized iron oilhouse was added in 1890 and a 2,000-gallon water tank placed near the barn.

In 1899 fortifications constructed nearby by the War Department necessitated the moving of Admiralty Head Light. In 1903 a new station replaced the one shown here. (Ca. 1890s photo by Herbert Bamber, National Archives #26-LG-61-10)

## Cleveland Harbor East Pier Light Station (1860, 1875)

Cleveland beacon, on the east pier (extending 600 feet into Lake Erie) at the entrance to Cleveland Harbor in Ohio, was established in 1831. Its lantern held four lamps with reflectors. In 1837 Lt. G. J. Pendergrast, U.S.N., wrote, "This is a point of great commercial importance, and has already a good artificial harbor, a light-house, and beacon. A beacon is all that is necessary, and I beg leave to advise that the light-house be discontinued."[99] In 1838 four lamps were added to the beacon. In 1854 a new lantern with a catadioptric apparatus of the fourth order was installed to distinguish its light from the many lights on the shore.[100] The east pier was extended 500 feet in 1860 and the wood octagonal tower shown on previous page was placed on it then. (1860 photo, National Archives #26-LG-44-60)

The lighthouse on the mainland of Cleveland Harbor was rebuilt in 1873. At that time the beacon was described as "being in a ruinous state, and having settled considerably to the east, should be rebuilt."[101] The beacon was rebuilt and lighted in 1875 with two fixed lights of the sixth order exhibited one above the other—the upper white, the lower red. In front of and connected with the beacon was a frame structure holding the fog bell struck by machinery. Mineral oil lamps were introduced in 1882. (1885 image below, National Archives #26-LG-44-49) In 1886 the white light was discontinued, with the red light placed in the upper position; the fog bell was discontinued and moved to the west breakwater in Cleveland Harbor, where a new light took precedence over the east pier. One keeper kept both lights, and in 1891 he was provided with a boathouse in front of the east pier light to shelter the boat he used to row to the west breakwater. By 1892 the *Annual Report* indicated that the east pier displayed only a masthead light. Both east pier and west breakwater were damaged when vessels ran into them in 1893. In 1897 a new concrete pier was completed on the east side of the harbor and a five-day lens lantern in an improved beacon was placed there.

Cleveland Harbor
East Pier Light
Station

THE U.S. LIGHT-HOUSE BOARD IMPROVES THE SYSTEM

## Navesink Light Station (1862)

Two light towers were first placed in 1828 on the Highlands of Navesink, New Jersey, to mark the western entrance to New York Bay. They were at an elevation of 250 feet. One of the first telegraphs was tested at this station. The Merchants Exchange of New York, having already placed a telegraph as part of its first system at Sandy Hook in 1827, proposed a second station at the more elevated Navesink in 1829:

> The importance of this facility of communication to the commerce of this country is a very obvious one, and to the Revenue of the United States is often equally essential. If a vessel is cast ashore and relief is not

speedily given, the cargo is plundered, and goes into the general consumption without paying duties; but by means of a rapid Telegraphic communication, assistance may be immediately rendered with a fair prospect that the property of individuals and the duties to the Government may be saved, and the lives of the persons on board preserved.[102]

In 1841 the twin towers were refitted with improved lenticular apparatus, one of the first order (fixed) and one of the second order (revolving)—the first test of this French invention in the United States. Their illumination was compared with that at Sandy Hook from ships several miles offshore and found to be an much as five times more powerful. Capt. H. K. Davenport, commanding the U. S. Mail Steamer *Cherokee*, wrote that "The Navesink lights are by far the best on our coast which have come under my observation, particularly the revolving light, which can be seen 25 miles."[103]

By 1857, however, the two towers were "in a dilapidated condition, the consequence of original bad materials and workmanship, . . . there is apprehension that they are not capable of standing much longer the heavy winter storms on the coast."[104] Two first-order light towers, one round, one octagonal, holding Fresnel lenses were authorized in 1861 and completed in 1862, as shown on page 165. The station then displayed two fixed lights of the first order, ending earlier confusion with the two lights on the Sandy Hook Lightship. The dwellings for the keepers were completed the following year. The ornate structure was justified as appealing to the many "citizens from all parts of the country who visit the station every year."[105]

In 1883 and 1884 the lard oil lamps were replaced with kerosene (mineral oil) lamps, the first use of mineral oil in a first-order lens in this country. An oil house to hold the very volatile fuel was built in 1890. Telephone connection with Fort Hancock and with the district engineer was established in 1898. That same year the fixed light in the south tower was replaced with a five-second-flash electric light—the first in an American lighthouse. Neighbors soon complained of the brilliancy of the flash. The keeper darkened three panels to accommodate them. In 1899 the light in the north tower was discontinued.

In 1954 the Navesink Lighthouse was turned over to the Borough of Highlands, New Jersey, as a historic site. (Photo on page 165 courtesy of the USCG Historian's Office)

THE U.S. LIGHT-HOUSE BOARD IMPROVES THE SYSTEM

# Cape Charles Light Station (1864, 1895)

In 1851, the 1828 tower on Cape Charles in Virginia was reported as "very inferior" and "requiring the earliest attention of the lighthouse department." The report further stated that, it "should be increased to a first order one."[106] A new 150-foot brick tower was begun in 1857 about one-and-a-quarter miles southwest of the 1828 tower. Construction on the tower was very slow and had progressed to only 83 feet in height by August 1863. At that time "the destruction by a party of armed men on the 3rd inst., of the [old tower] illuminating apparatus at Cape Charles (Smith Island) and the probable destruction of other lights in that vicinity" was reported. "A Notice to Mariners of this depredation" was published.[107]

Keeper Grose wrote in February 1864 to the lighthouse engineer complaining of the conduct of soldiers stationed to protect the site. After cleaning up after the previous military party, a party of 25 soldiers (contrabands) with two commissioned officers arrived and immediately took possession of one of the keeper's dwellings. Grose wrote, "The soldiers are quite misplaced where they have posted themselves, evidently having only the idea of making comfortable quarters."

The district engineer reported that

> The question of the Military Guard on this island has been from the commencement quite vexatious. They are amenable to no discipline. Their dilapidations and injury to Government property exceed all that has been done by the rebels; and now just as things are being straightened up and the work proceeded with, a party of contrabands, fresh, as Mr. Grose states is reported to him, from a small-pox-infected district, arrive to upset the arrangements and scare the men out of all reason.

Another letter dated February 16, 1864, quotes keeper Grose:

> The Corps d'Afrique are destroying Government property; they have burned lumber and about 200 wedges. [Wedges were used in the repairs of the tramway.] . . .They are insulting in their manners. They have destroyed all the water fit for use, and which would have lasted my party for months. . . . They take possession of, and use, whatever they wish for, and the man claiming to be Capt of the Guard [?] says that he has command of the Island and that I must not only submit to but obey him. . . . They are tearing what is left of the barracks to pieces, and upon my offer to repair it, (the barracks) if they would move out of the keepers house, the answer was: <u>No</u> [sic]. . . . I have also been threatened with arrest and conveyance to jail.[108]

The tower was finally completed on May 7, 1864, and outfitted with a first-order lens. (Photo on page 167 courtesy of the USCG Historian's Office)

A third tower was built at Cape Charles when the shoreline had eroded to the point that the sea encroached upon the old tower. A 191-foot-tall cast-iron pyramidal skeletal tower shown opposite, the tallest of its type, was completed on December 21, 1894, and commissioned on August 15, 1895. (Courtesy of the USCG Historian's Office) The station continues as an active aid to navigation.

THE U.S. LIGHT-HOUSE BOARD IMPROVES THE SYSTEM

Cape Charles Light Station

# Fort Point Light Station (1864)

Built at the same time as Alcatraz, the second lighthouse on the West Coast was completed in 1853 at the entrance to San Francisco Bay, but immediately torn down to make room for Fort Winfield Scott. In 1855 a four-sided, truncated wooden tower, equipped with a fifth-order lens, was constructed on a narrow ledge outside the fort. An inadequate fog bell was mounted on the side of the fort, just under the mouths of cannons, reached by an open ladder down the side wall.[109]

On April 4, 1861, a letter to the Secretary of the Treasury presented a problem:

> The necessity for the change of position [of the Fort Point Light] has become more apparent within the last few days; previous to the 22nd of February, the Fort was for the first time occupied by troops and on that day a national salute was fired from it, the concussion caused by the successive discharges shattered all the window glass, and also the clock in the cleaning room.[110]

During the Civil War erosion of the sea wall forced the removal of that lighthouse as well.

In 1864 the iron-skeletal light tower shown below was erected over the stairway of the fort's northwest corner and bolted to the fort's stone roof. (National Archives #26-LG-64-42B) A fourth-order lens was revolved by a

The U.S. Light-House Board Improves the System

clockwork drive that required rewinding every two and one-half hours. The keepers lived in houses located on the bluff just south of the fort as shown in photo above. (National Archives #26-LG-66-2) The buildings were anchored to the ground with cables to resist the powerful winds that funnel through the Golden Gate. Reaching the light tower with the wind blowing at hurricane force sorely tried the keepers. Fort Point Keeper James Rankin (1878-1919) became famous for making 18 daring rescues from the sea wall in front of the fort.

The construction of the Golden Gate Bridge, directly over the lighthouse, reduced its utility. The light and foghorn were relocated offshore on one of the main bridge piers. The lighthouse ceased operation in 1934. In 1970 the Fort Point National Historic Site, including a restored Fort Point Light, was established by the National Park Service.

## SIDEBAR: Lighthouse/Buoy Tenders

In the first half of the nineteenth century, revenue cutters were generally responsible for tending the buoys and providing transportation of officials to the light stations; although harbor pilots were often paid to set and establish bouys. Contracts were let for supplying oil and other provisions required to light the lamps and to keep them in repair. At some isolated stations, visits from a representative of the Lighthouse Establishment were fairly infrequent. Many of the revenue cutters were hard pressed to tend the increasing number of buoys in and out of their regular domain. Local collectors began to lobby for a vessel specifically for the needs of aids in their region. In 1843, Pleasonton agreed that some adjustments in the system for tending buoys was called for.

> I have the honor to observe, that I have found no part of the Light House service more vexatious and difficult of execution than providing, mooring, and keeping the Buoys in their proper stations, dispersed as they are along the Coast, and in the Bays, from Maine to Louisiana, and I may add, in the Lakes also. To the South, it is almost impossible, after Buoys are provided and stationed, to keep them up. There are neither Buoys nor vessels to be had to replace such as are carried away by storms, which are of frequent occurrence. I am therefore obliged to send to Boston for all, or nearly all, that are wanted for South Carolina and Georgia, and employ the Cutter in mooring them, and this produces delay which is vexatious and injurious to the navigating interest.[111]

Pharos, *an example of a tender powered by sail. (National Archives #26-LSH-38-1)*

THE U.S. LIGHT-HOUSE BOARD IMPROVES THE SYSTEM

Jessamine *(top), built in 1881 (1885 photo by Major Jared A. Smith, National Archives #26-LSH-32A-3).* *The Light-House Board also owned several supply vessels and tugs such as* Thistle *(bottom) (National Archives #26-LSH-41-1).*

Pleasonton mentioned that in New York Bay, the pilots had been contracted to tend the buoys, the cutters being opposed to performing that duty. In 1839 a condemned cutter was made seaworthy for the purpose of taking care of the buoys and conveying oil, etc., to the lighthouses and lightships in the New York district. In Delaware Bay, a vessel was chartered to perform these services. In the Chesapeake Bay, where the Revenue Cutters "do not consider the taking up and mooring Buoys, conveying oil, etc., to the Light Boats, a fit service for them,"[112] Pleasonton suggested that a vessel be built or chartered for the task, thus confining the duties of the cutters to "subjecting their officers to an occasional examination of the Light Houses."[113] In the waters of South Carolina and Georgia, the small number of buoys did not warrant the expense of hiring a separate vessel for their care.

In the second half of the nineteenth century, the U.S. Light-House Board, from the beginning of its jurisdiction, saw the need for more visits to the lighthouses:

> Instead of, as now, employing on the Atlantic coast two sailing vessels, for nearly the entire year, in making one visit to each light, the same service could be much more effectively and economically performed by a small steamer, which could visit every light on the entire Atlantic coast three times during the year; thus affording the keepers opportunities of making known their wants and complaints, and at the same time exert a salutary influence upon the keepers, by pointing out defects in the management of the establishments.[114]

Gradually, most lighthouse districts owned at least one tender for tending buoys, some powered by sail, others by steam. Tenders also carried inspectors to the stations or were used in construction or repair at the stations. Soon vessels were specifically designed for tending buoys. Tenders resembled the sleek revenue cutters or, in some cases, large seagoing tugs. The first steam tender, *Shubrick*, was a sidewheel steamer built in 1857 for use on the Pacific coast. By 1887, steam had replaced sail as the standard method of propulsion.

## SIDEBAR: Lighthouse Depots

After dividing the country into districts, the Light-House Board provided each district with one to five depots to supply the stations and to serve as a base for tending the other aids to navigation. Each depot had a dock for supply vessels and buoy tenders and a storehouse. Many also had fuel houses; work space for lampists, machinists, carpenters, and blacksmiths; housing for the depot keeper; and storage for lumber, coal, paint, oil, buoys, sinkers, chains, and other supplies. Often the relief lightship was moored at a depot. Construction crews generally operated out of depots. These crews not only constructed new aids to navigation, but also undertook any major repairs required at the stations.[115]

A central depot located at Thompkinsville on Staten Island, New York, was constructed soon after the Civil War. Not only did this facility transfer supplies, Fresnel lenses, and oil to the district depots, but it also tested new equipment and experimented with evolving technology. The Light-House Board justified the new depot in its 1867 *Annual Report*:

> Previous to the establishment of this depot the reserve material for the light-house service was stored in several districts, involving the necessity for a multiplication of storage buildings, mechanics, workmen, supplies of all kinds, apparatus, etc., and it frequently happened that articles were purchased for use in one district when there was an excess of the same in other districts. To reduce to the minimum the supply of the service and the consequent expense, it was evident that there must be one storehouse, one workshop, one oil vault, etc., gathered together at one spot and called a depot, from which all needed

*Experimental lighthouse in front of one of the Staten Island Depot piers. (National Archives #26-LG-15-59)*

supplies and apparatus could be issued as they might be wanted, upon requisitions from the inspectors or engineers of the several districts, approved at the office of the Light-House Board. For convenience of purchase and shipment, it was just as evident that this depot must be at or in the immediate vicinity of New York city. . . .

The depot . . . very soon proved its usefulness, even far beyond what had been anticipated, and its convenience and economy were fully equal to its usefulness. Although it was expected that the business of the depot would be large, it has far exceeded the expectations, and it was demonstrated that there was neither sufficient room nor facilities to insure the best practical results or to answer all the demands made upon the depot; and under authority of an act of Congress appropriating requisite amount therefore, a strip of land on the north side of the lot was purchased from the State of New York. . . .

To render the harbor perfectly safe for the mooring during winter of the tenders and spare vessels of the establishment, very considerable improvement will be necessary, but it is not proposed to make them during the next season, therefore no appropriation is required at present.

Arrangements have been made at this depot for testing oils offered by contractors and for experimenting with lamps, apparatus, etc., used in the service. These arrangements are yet limited, but will be extended in accordance with results obtained.[116]

In 1998, the Staten Island Depot was selected as the site for the National Lighthouse Museum and Center.

*Staten Island Depot Lamp Shop crew ca. 1890 (National Archives #26-LG-16-7)*

THE U.S. LIGHT-HOUSE BOARD IMPROVES THE SYSTEM

Point Lookout was chosen for the site of a buoy depot in 1883 because it was ideally situated between the Lazeretto Depot in Baltimore to the north and the Portsmouth Depot in Norfolk to the south. The depot, built next to the Point Lookout Lighthouse, served to store, repair, and place buoys in the middle portion of the Chesapeake Bay. The keeper, with additional pay, was placed in charge of both the lighthouse and the depot. A tramway with two cars was added in 1885 for moving supplies, buoys, and coal between the sheds and the wharf where tenders would pick up and drop off buoys. (Photo taken by Major Jared A. Smith in 1885, National Archives #26-LG-24-8)

FOUNDATION
Sectional Elevation on Line AA [Plate 3].

*Construction of Spectacle Reef Light Station in Michigan. (National Archives, RG 26)*

THE U.S. LIGHT-HOUSE BOARD ACHIEVES ITS GOALS

# IV. The U.S. Light-House Board Achieves Its Goals

The construction of lighthouses on the Great Lakes, often referred to as the "Northern Lakes," increased with the burgeoning of commerce in that area. In addition to lighthouses built on land, many were built on pierheads. Up to 1883, more money was spent in placing lights on the waters of the State of Michigan than any other state on ocean, gulf, or lake. Most ships on the Lakes navigated close to land; because vessels never traveled far offshore, aids with shorter ranges were adequate. Conditions, however, were difficult; entrances to ports are often shallow, fog abounds in spring and fall, fierce storms are frequent, and numerous island and shoals present hazards.[1]

Wooden cribs were used as a foundation type for many offshore lighthouses in the Great Lakes. The crib was constructed onshore, towed to the site, and then filled with stone to sink it in place. Once settled and leveled, the cribs were capped with concrete or some other masonry upon which the lighthouse was constructed. Many crib lighthouses with granite foundations used a temporary cofferdam to construct the foundations. Usually made of wood and partially assembled on shore, the cofferdam was brought to the site, bolted together, sealed, and the water pumped out. Once the foundation was constructed safely above the water level, the cofferdam was dismantled, and the lighthouse tower built on top of the foundation.

Under the Light-House Board, the appointment of keepers was restricted to

> persons between the ages of 18 and 50, who can read, write, and keep accounts, are able to do the requisite manual labor, to pull and sail a boat, and have enough mechanical ability to make necessary minor repairs about the premises, and keep them painted, whitewashed, and in order.[2]

Keepers underwent a three-month probationary period before their full appointment was issued by the Secretary of Treasury. Keepers could be transferred between stations and districts. Young men with some sea experience were preferred as assistants at the larger stations, while retired sea captains or mates with families were frequently selected for stations with only one keeper. Stations with fog signals generally required an assistant with some experience as a machinist to operate the machinery and keep it in repair.[3] In 1867, an Act of Congress fixed the average salary of a lighthouse keeper at $600.[4]

## SIDEBAR: Illuminants

The Fresnel lens used less oil than the earlier reflector apparatus; however, the price of sperm oil continued to rise with diminishing whale catches and increase in use of sperm oil as a lubricant. After unsuccessful experiments with colza or vegetable oil in the early 1860s, lard oil was found to produce an adequate light at a cost savings. A few decades later, when further economy was required, mineral oil or kerosene replaced lard oil, and a new lamp invented specifically for it came into use. By 1885, kerosene was the principal illuminant and was used in Incandescent Oil Vapor (IOV) Lamps. Because it was highly combustible, separate oil houses were required to house the kerosene. Natural gas was also tested as an illuminant but was not widely adopted. In the late 1880s, the use of electricity as an illuminant was first tried in several aids, including the Sandy Hook East Beacon and the Statue of Liberty in New York Harbor.[5]

*Sandy Hook East Beacon (1867) at the entrance to New York Bay in New Jersey. (National Archives #26-LG-15-7)*

The U.S. Light-House Board organized the country into 12 lighthouse districts in 1852. Later, districts were added to cover the inland waters and boundaries were reconfigured so that by the end of the century, 16 districts existed to cover aids to navigation in the United States. Each district had an inspector, a Navy officer charged with the maintenance of the lights and lighthouses as well as the discipline of the keepers. The district engineer, an army officer, was charged with building the lighthouses and keeping them in repair as well as the purchase, installation, and maintenance of the illuminating apparatus.[7]

| | 1867 | 1877 | 1887 | 1897 |
|---|---|---|---|---|
| **First District:** | | | | |
| Maine through New Hampshire | | | | |
| Lighthouses & Lighted Beacons | 46 | 54 | 54 | 68 |
| Lightships | | | | |
| Unlighted Beacons | 41 | 71 | 95 | 103 |
| Buoys in Position | 303 | 410 | 531 | 701 |
| Tenders/Supply Vessels | 1 | 3 | 2 | 2 |
| **Second District:**[8] | | | | |
| Hampton Harbor, New Hampshire, through Massachusetts | | | | |
| Lighthouses & Lighted Beacons | 63 | 62 | 64 | 79 |
| Lightships | 7 | 10 | 8 | 10 |
| Unlighted Beacons | 50 | 51 | 58 | 74 |
| Buoys in Position | 451 | 432 | 480 | 548 |
| Tenders/Supply Vessels | 2 | 2 | 3 | 4 |
| **Third District:**[9] | | | | |
| Gooseberry Point, Massachusetts, to Squam Inlet, New Jersey | | | | |
| Lighthouses & Lighted Beacons | 92 | 122 | 155 | 248[10] |
| Lightships | 6 | 9 | 7 | 8 |
| Unlighted Beacons | 44 | 39 | 44 | 38 |
| Buoys in Position | 335 | 417 | 523 | 633 |
| Tenders/Supply Vessels | 2 | 5 | 5 | 8 |
| **Fourth District:** | | | | |
| Squam Inlet, New Jersey, through Metomkin Inlet, Virginia | | | | |
| Lighthouses & Lighted Beacons | 18 | 32 | 49 | 63[11] |
| Lightships | 2 | 4 | 3 | 4 |
| Unlighted Beacons | 2 | | 2 | 5 |
| Buoys in Position | 75 | 131 | 168 | 212 |
| Tenders | 1 | 2 | 1 | 2 |

| | 1867 | 1877 | 1887 | 1897 |
|---|---|---|---|---|
| **Fifth District:** | | | | |
| Metomkin Inlet, Virginia, through New River Inlet, North Carolina | | | | |
| Lighthouses & Lighted Beacons | 62 | 71 | 96 | 126[12] |
| Lightships | 4 | | | |
| Unlighted Beacons | 85 | 69 | 13 | 10 |
| Buoys in Position | 460 | 689 | 1011 | 1154 |
| Tenders | 2 | 3 | 8 | 6 |
| **Sixth District:**[13] | | | | |
| New River Inlet, North Carolina, through Cape Canaveral, Florida | | | | |
| Lighthouses & Lighted Beacons | 49 | 35 | 123 | 204[14] |
| Lightships | 5 | 5 | 3 | 3 |
| Unlighted Beacons | 123 | 75 | 29 | 41 |
| Buoys in Position | 146 | 262 | 282 | 306 |
| Tenders | 2 | 3 | 2 | 4 |
| **Seventh District:**[15] | | | | |
| Cape Canaveral, Florida, through Perdido River, Florida | | | | |
| Lighthouses & Lighted Beacons | 10 | 17 | 20 | 53 |
| Lightships | None | | | |
| Unlighted Beacons | 18 | 60 | 27 | 35 |
| Buoys in Position | 57 | 144 | 203 | 269 |
| Tenders | 1 | 3 | 3 | 3 |
| **Eighth District:** | | | | |
| Perdido River, Florida, through Rio Grande, Texas | | | | |
| Lighthouses & Lighted Beacons | 64 | 45 | 54 | 91 |
| Lightships | | 1 | 2 | 2 |
| Unlighted Beacons | 41 | 8 | 13 | 14 |
| Buoys in Position | 80 | 93 | 92 | 224 |
| Tenders | 3 | 2 | 3 | 3 |
| **Ninth District:** | | | | |
| Lake Michigan, Green Bay, and waters west of the Straits of Mackinac | | | | |
| Lighthouses & Lighted Beacons | | | 70 | 102 |
| Lightships | | | 4 | |
| Unlighted Beacons | | | | |
| Buoys in Position | | | 49 | 105 |
| Tenders | | | 1 | 4 |

THE U.S. LIGHT-HOUSE BOARD ACHIEVES ITS GOALS

|  | 1867 | 1877 | 1887 | 1897 |
|---|---|---|---|---|
| **Tenth District:** | | | | |
| Mouth of St. Regis River, New York, to Grassy Island, Detroit River, Michigan | | | | |
| Lighthouses & Lighted Beacons | 44 | 60 | 70 | 77 |
| Lightships | | | | 4 |
| Unlighted Beacons | | 1 | | |
| Buoys in Position | 79 | 102 | 167 | 150 |
| Tenders | 1 | 1 | 1 | 1 |
| **Eleventh District:** | | | | |
| Lake Region above Grassy Island, Michigan | | | | |
| Lighthouses & Lighted Beacons | 63 | 120 | 77 | 198[16] |
| Lightships | | | 1 | 3 |
| Unlighted Beacons | | 1 | 1 | 1 |
| Buoys in Position | 80 | 151 | 136 | 376 |
| Tenders | 1 | 2 | 1 | 4 |
| **Twelfth District:** | | | | |
| California | | | | |
| Lighthouses & Lighted Beacons | 9 | 22 | 22 | 39 |
| Lightships | | | | |
| Unlighted Beacons | | 28 | 41 | 54 |
| Buoys in Position | | 27 | 64 | 89 |
| Tenders | | 1 | 1 | 3 |
| **Thirteenth District:** | | | | |
| Oregon and Washington | | | | |
| Lighthouses & Lighted Beacons | 9 | 11 | 45[17] | 127[18] |
| Lightships | | | | 1 |
| Unlighted Beacons | | 18 | 38 | 44 |
| Buoys in Position[19] | | 82 | 176 | 283 |
| Tenders | | 1 | 1 | 2 |

Note: Many of the tenders served more than one district.

Keepers were encouraged to cultivate the land associated with onshore stations and were forbidden to engage in any business that interfered with their presence at the station or with the proper and timely performance of their duties. It was not surprising, however, to find a keeper working at his station as a shoemaker, tailor, or a justice of the peace. Keepers were not allowed to take in boarders nor were they given pensions or compensation for injury. In 1883 male keepers were issued uniforms consisting of a coat, vest, trousers, and a cap in a dark indigo blue color. The 1885 *Annual Report* stated, "It is believed that uniforming the personnel of the service, some 1,600 in number, will aid in maintaining its discipline, increase its efficiency, raise its tone, and add to its esprit de corps." A regulation apron was to be worn during inside cleaning and a brown working suit for outdoor work.

Keepers were encouraged to "consider the care of the light and the light-house property their paramount duty, beyond any personal consideration."[20] Stories of heroism in the line of duty have become an integral part of lighthouse lore.

Inspectors visited the stations in their districts quarterly. They were to report on repairs needed to the tower and buildings; needed renovations and improvements; condition of the station, lantern, illuminating apparatus, and related equipment. Comparisons were made of the interval of flashes and eclipses and their duration, with the intervals given in the *Light List*. The inspector was responsible for making sure the keeper understood the printed instructions for operating all equipment and other attendant duties. The inspector also reviewed the keeper's journal and records relating to expenditures, shipwrecks, and vessels passing. The inspector

assessed the "attention of the keeper to his duties, and his ability to perform them well."[21] Both inspectors and engineers had authority to dismiss a keeper or other employee found in a state of intoxication.

Engineers superintended the "construction and renovation of the fixed aids to navigation in their respective districts."[22] The engineer or the inspector was responsible for acquiring information on the ownership of any potential site and reporting these details to the Board along with information about the topography of the site and the potential light's relationship with other lights and the water or hazard it was marking. Engineers were instructed to inspect all materials and supplies to make sure they were in conformance with contracts. When a tower was nearing completion, the engineer notified the superintendent of lights so that he could nominate the authorized number of keepers.

Superintendents of lights were charged with paying salaries and dispersing other funds, as well as nominating light-keepers. Keepers were allowed to select their assistants; however, the superintendent was responsible for nominating the candidate for the appointment.

Aids to navigation were distinguished by their "shape, arrangement, and color, according to the peculiarity of the respective localities, the kind of background, and the characteristic features of adjacent structures."[23] To preserve the overall appearance of a site, an old tower or building was removed when a replacement was erected. New buildings could not be erected, colors of buildings changed, or trees cut down without the authority of the Board. Lights were initially classified according to six orders; the strongest or first order were placed on important headlands, and the smallest were used to mark bays, sounds, or obstructions in rivers, or on piers or wharves.

The U.S. Light-House Board Achieves Its Goals

There were four orders of lanterns based on uniform plans. First-, second-, and third-order lanterns were used for corresponding orders of lenses. The fourth-order lantern was used for fourth-, fifth-, and sixth-order lenses. Lighthouse towers were designed to support a specific order of lens and lantern.

The 1875 *Annual Report* reported that it was time to provide keepers with reading matter. "By so doing, keepers will be made happier and more contented with their lot, and less desirous of absenting themselves from their post." By 1884, 380 libraries were being circulated amongst the stations. In 1896, lighthouse service employees were classified within the federal civil service system.

---

## SIDEBAR: Instructions to Employees of the Lighthouse Service, 1881

The newly formed Light-House Board stressed the importance of the written instructions in its 1852 report. "Inspectors and light-keepers should be provided with printed instructions, in the form of manuals of instruction, as well as those necessary to guide them in the policing of the establishments, similar to those provided for inspectors of light-houses in France and Great Britain."

The *1881 Instructions* began, "The Keeper is responsible for the care and management of the light, and for the station in general. He must enforce a careful attention to duty on the part of his assistants; and the assistants are strictly enjoined to render prompt obedience to his lawful orders." Absences were to be communicated to those left in charge and reported to the inspector. "Light-keepers may leave their stations to attend divine worship on Sundays, to procure needful supplies, and on important public occasions."

"Watches must be kept at all stations where there is an assistant. The keeper on watch must remain in the watch room and give continuous attention to the light while he is on duty. When there is no assistant, the keeper must visit the light at least twice during the night between 8 p.m. and sunrise; and on stormy nights the light must be constantly looked after."

A keeper was expected to understand how to operate the apparatus and use strict economy in the use of his supplies: "He must be careful to prevent waste, theft, or misapplication of light house property." Quantities of oil and other supplies used each day were to be recorded.

"Light-keepers must not engage in any traffic on light-house premises, and they must not permit it by any one else. They must not carry on any business or trade elsewhere which will cause them to be often absent from the premises, or to neglect, in any way, their proper duties."

Visitors to the light station were to be treated courteously and politely, but not allowed to handle the apparatus or carve their names on the lantern glass or tower windows. Intoxicated persons were to be removed "by the employment of all proper and reasonable means."

Keepers were not to change the color of towers or buildings without written orders. All parts of the station, including bed chambers, were to be neatly kept. "Untidiness will be strongly reprehended, and its continuance will subject a keeper to dismissal."

Shipwrecks were to be reported promptly to the inspector. "It is the duty of light-keepers to aid wrecked persons as far as lies in their power." Precautions were to be taken against fire; fire-buckets were to be kept filled and ready. Burning mineral oil, or kerosene, was to be extinguished with sand or ashes rather than water.

Boats were furnished at stations where they were "necessary for communication with the mainland, to obtain household supplies, etc." They were to be used only for light-house purposes; "the boats must not be used for freighting, wrecking, fishing with seines, ferrying, or for carrying goods or passengers for hire."

Paperwork increased for the keepers. They were to submit monthly reports on the condition of the station and make explicit specification for any needed repairs. A monthly report on the fog signal and absences from the station was also required. Expenditures of oil, etc., and salary vouchers were to be submitted quarterly. Property returns were submitted annually as well as receipts for extra supplies, the keeper's receipt for property on taking charge, receipts for delivery of supplies, shipwreck reports, and reports of any damage to station or apparatus and any unusual occurrence were made as necessary. The keepers were expected to keep a daily-expenditure book, a general-account book, and a journal. This journal, or log, must record the events of the day in one line written across two pages. "The visits of the Inspector or Engineer, or of the lampist or machinist, and an account of any work going on or delivery of stores must be noted; as also any item of interest occurring in the vicinity, such as the state of the weather, or other similar matter. The books must be kept in ink, with neatness, and must always be kept up to date."

Special instructions were provided to keepers of stations where navigation was closed down by ice in winter. "Lights may be extinguished when navigation is entirely suspended, but must always be shown if it is at all possible for vessels to benefit by them." Keepers at island stations who could not remain there during the winter "must continue their lights as long as possible in the fall without endangering their lives by being caught in the ice; and must return to their stations as early in the spring as the ice will permit."

A section devoted to the "Care of Lights and their Appurtenances" included detailed instructions on the care of the optics. The keepers were to hang lantern curtains each morning and to wear a linen apron to protect the lens "from contact with the wearing apparel." The lens and lantern glass were to be cleaned daily. Rouge was used to polish the lens and "rotten-stone" to shine the brass. "Keepers are forbidden to use any other materials for cleaning and polishing than those supplied by the Light-house Establishment." The revolving clockwork and carriage rollers were to be kept properly oiled. Keepers were to cut replacement glass for the lantern when necessary.

Other sections were devoted to care and management of other equipment, particularly the fog signal, and specific instructions were provided for the keepers of lightships. The last section listed "Allowances of Provisions" for unusually isolated stations, amended in 1883:

| | | | |
|---|---|---|---|
| Beef | 200 pounds | Potatoes | 4 bushels |
| Pork | 100 pounds | Onions | 1 bushel |
| Flour | 1 barrel | Sugar | 50 pounds |
| Rice | 25 pounds | Coffee | 24 pounds |
| Beans | 10 gallons | Vinegar | 4 gallons |

Caisson construction was first used in building supports for bridges. A caisson foundation for lighthouses utilized a cast-iron-plate cylinder. The cylinder was pre-assembled onshore to ensure proper fitting. Depending on bottom conditions and depth of water, the cylinder was fitted with either a temporary watertight bottom or a permanent wooden crib. The cylinder was towed to its desired location and sunk by controlled flooding of the interior achieved through a valve located in the chamber and/or by ballasting.[24] Once the cylinder was leveled, riprap stone was added around the outside to add stability and prevent bottom scour by currents. Then the sand and mud within the cylinder were pumped out. Water hoses or jets were sometimes used to clear debris around the outside of the cylinder to assist in the settling of the assembly. More stone and concrete were added to assist in the settling. Additional plates could be added to the cylinder as it settled in order for it to reach the desired height above the water surface.[25]

On top of the caisson, a cast-iron or brick lighthouse tower and integral keeper's quarters were built. A cellar was often built inside the caisson foundation and used for storing wood or coal and for cisterns to hold water collected through the roof gutter and downspout system.

The first level above the foundation contained the entrance. It was usually partitioned into a sitting room, kitchen, and storage area, and completely surrounded by a gallery. The second, and sometimes a third, floor was dedicated to sleeping areas and storage. The level directly below the lantern was the watch room.[26]

Caissons were sometimes employed where solid bottoms could not be obtained by dredging or other means. The caisson lighthouse type was sturdier and better able to withstand the stresses exerted by ice flow that played havoc with the screwpile structures. Many damaged screwpile lighthouses were replaced with caisson-type structures; the caisson structures, however, were far more expensive to construct. They were built from the northern coast of Maine to the Chesapeake Bay. The beginning of the end of

*Foundation cylinder for cast-iron caisson for the 1874 Ship John Shoal Light Station in Delaware, onshore. (National Archives #26-LG-21-46)*

*Caisson for Ship John Shoal Light Station being towed to the site where it was sunk into the bay bottom, then filled with concrete. (National Archives #26-LG-21-47)*

screwpile cottage-type lighthouses came in 1894 when the Light-House Board stated in its *Annual Report*,

> In view of recent damages by ice to screwpile structures in Chesapeake Bay, the Board is now of the opinion that only caisson structures should be used where such dangers exist.[27]

The only one of the many screwpile lighthouses to remain intact in its original location is Thomas Point Shoal; most caisson structures survive.

Toward the end of the nineteenth century, a pneumatic caisson technique was developed for use where bottoms were harder or contained rocks, and/or where greater depth of penetration into the substrate was desired. A wooden, open-ended, box-like crib contraption called the caisson was attached to the bottom of the cast-iron-plated cylinder with the open side of the box facing down. Typically the timbers forming the caisson were one foot square. The entire caisson was sheathed and sealed with mineral pitch to make it essentially watertight. In later years the caisson was occasionally made of steel. The lower sides or rim of the caisson were tapered near the bottom to ease the settling of the caisson into the bottom sediments. Water was forced out of the caisson by means of pressurized air. The tubular cylinder fitted on top of the caisson was then partially filled with cement. The added weight further settled the assembly into the substrate.[28]

An airtight shaft built in the center of the assembly (caisson and attached cylinder) was big enough for men to climb up and down. It provided access to the caisson where they would haul out, or suck out with hoses, the debris from inside the bottom of the caisson. Removal of these bottom sediments allowed the assembly to slowly sink further into the bottom, typically about one to two feet a day. The digging continued until the caisson had sunk to the desired depth, usually about 30 feet into the substrate. The contraption was also outfitted with an air-lock to maintain the needed air pressure to keep water out of the caisson as well as an air pipe to the surface to maintain fresh air supplies. Once this work was completed the air chamber in the caisson was completely filled with compacted sand and the air and worker access shafts were filled with concrete. The first pneumatic caisson lighthouse built in the United States was Fourteen Foot Bank Lighthouse (1887) in Delaware.[29] Eleven pneumatic caisson lighthouses were built in the United States.

THE U.S. LIGHT-HOUSE BOARD ACHIEVES ITS GOALS

*Bloody Point Bar Light Station (1882), an example of a caisson lighthouse with a cast-iron tower, often referred to as a "sparkplug." (1885 photo by Major Jared Smith courtesy of the USCG Historian's Office)*

# Newport Harbor (Goat Island) Light Station (1865)

An octagonal lighthouse was established in 1823 on the north end of Goat Island at the entrance to Newport Harbor in Rhode Island. In 1838 it was replaced by a lighthouse on the nearby breakwater. Captain Connor of the Revenue Cutter *Jackson* reported in 1843 that Goat Island is "a good and safe mark to guide vessels into the Harbour of Newport—by keeping Beavertail and Goat Island in range you avoid all danger."[30] In 1851 the tower was disassembled and moved to Prudence Island, where another tower had been swept away in a storm.

THE U.S. LIGHT-HOUSE BOARD ACHIEVES ITS GOALS

In 1865 the octagonal tower of rough-cut granite with attached dwelling shown opposite was built on the breakwater on Goat Island. Its fog bell was struck by machinery every 15 seconds. The light was automated in 1963. The tower still stands and is an active aid to navigation, but a submarine struck the keeper's quarters in 1922 and damaged it so badly that it was town down. (National Archives #26-LG-6-79)

## Ediz Hook Light Station (1865)

Ediz Hook, a point of land in False Dungeness Bay in the Strait of Juan de Fuca, Washington Territory, had a temporary light, privately maintained, in 1863. A federal lighthouse was completed and lighted there in 1865. In 1880 mineral oil lamps were substituted for the lard oil previously used. A brick oil house for storing fuel was added the following year. A 3,000-pound fog bell, struck by machinery, in a pyramid-shaped tower 320 feet from the lighthouse, was added in 1886. In 1893 the Port Angeles Mill and Lumber Company, which had been illegally occupying part of the reservation for several years, was evicted. The 1865 tower was replaced with a newer tower in 1909, sold, and barged across the harbor to become a private residence. (Courtesy of the USCG Historian's Office)

## Mamajuda Light Station (1866)

The Mamajuda Light Station was established on the Detroit River, Michigan, in 1849. An examination in 1865 found it necessary to rebuild the station, "the present structures not being thought worthy of the repairs required to make them habitable."

After the Civil War a disabled veteran of the Union Army, Barney Litogot, was appointed keeper. He died in 1873 as "the result of wounds received . . . during the war of the rebellion."[31] The Superintendent recommended that his wife Caroline be appointed to replace him. "She is worthy and needy, having a family of children to support, and left penniless . . ." Caroline received the appointment and served until 1885.

An 1898 letter describes the station as being "built on pilings and surrounded by a platform with a walk to the island." Local fishermen used the island to raise a garden. "The portion which is not cultivated is kept in a very unsightly condition, old buildings and refuse of many kinds being strewn over it. The keeper has at times tried to clean up the portion nearest his dwelling, but has been stopped by the fishermen who claimed he was interfering to make them trouble."[32]

The station is no longer extant. (National Archives #26-LG-51-13)

# Plattsburg Breakwater Light Station (1867)

The 1867 *Annual Report* reported as follows on Plattsburg Breakwater Light Station on Lake Champlain in New York State:

> Owing to the damaged condition of the north end of the breakwater, the lighted beacon at the south end only could be erected. A steamer lens was exhibited on this beacon on the evening of August 1, 1867. The repair to the north end of the breakwater . . . will soon be finished. The frame of the beacon for the north end is ready for erection, and the lantern has been delivered.

In 1886 the color of the lights was changed from white to fixed red to keep them from being confused with the electric lights behind them in the town. In 1893 the beacon was removed to the extreme end of the extended breakwater, but does not survive. (National Archives #26-LG-13-47)

# Cape Canaveral Light Station (1868)

Local builders put up a 60-foot tower on Cape Canaveral on the Florida coast in 1848, but mariners immediately complained that they had to sail too close to shore to see the light.[33] The countryside was not yet settled, for Stephen Pleasonton wrote to the Secretary of the Treasury on August 1, 1849, as follows:

> I have the honor to enclose a letter from . . . the keeper at Cape Canaveral Light, by which you will perceive the Keeper considers himself and family in danger from hostile Indians in his neighborhood, and requests to be furnished with a guard of 10 men.
>
> As we have no money applicable to such a purpose, and this light, as well as that at Cape Florida, will be abandoned if a guard is not furnished at each place, I respectfully submit the propriety of calling upon the War Department to furnish such a guard.
>
> In the war of 1836 with these Indians, the Light House at Cape Florida was burnt by these Indians, one keeper killed, and another badly wounded. Hence it is probable that neither this Keeper, nor the one at Cape Canaveral, will remain at their respective lights, if a guard sufficient to ensure their safety be not furnished.[34]

A small contingent of soldiers was sent, one of whom, Henry Wilson, married the daughter of the second keeper, Capt. Mills Olcott Burnham, a Vermonter. Wilson left the army, became assistant keeper at Canaveral, and then keeper in 1885 after Burnham's death. He was succeeded in 1887 by another son-in-law of Burnham's.

The 1857 *Annual Report* described dangerous shoals that extended 12 miles offshore from Cape Canaveral in Florida and caused numerous shipwrecks. "A light should be at least 150 feet high to be of any use to navigators." Construction of a new tower was begun, but then suspended when the Civil War broke out. Keeper Mills Burnham, appointed in 1853, had the lamp and clockworks packed in wooden cases for safekeeping and abandoned the station. He was reappointed when the war ended and served until he died of measles in 1885.[35]

Work resumed in 1867, and the new tower was completed in 1868, 139 feet above sea level. "The structure was of cast-iron sections lined with brick, with iron bands extending through from the outside at every eight feet."[36] The lantern held a first-order lens that cost $50,000 and revolved by a weight-driven clockwork.

Assistant keepers were supposed to live in the tower, but the excessive heat led them to build sheds nearby. A hurricane in 1876 destroyed all the

THE U.S. LIGHT-HOUSE BOARD ACHIEVES ITS GOALS

outbuildings. The keeper's dwelling shown here was erected in 1878; assistant keeper's quarters were built in 1883. (National Archives #26-LG-26-24)

In 1894 continuing erosion prompted the dismantling of the tower and the moving of the whole station a mile further inland to its present location. Since 1950 the Cape Canaveral light has been witness to the United States space program. This tower is still an active aid to navigation, displaying a DCB 224 modern beacon light; the first-order Fresnel lens is on display at the Ponce de Leon Lighthouse Museum.

## SIDEBAR: Screwpile Lighthouses in the James River

In 1855 lights were established at several sites on the James River in Virginia, all of them screwpile structures with large pressed-glass masthead lenses suspended in the lantern. During the Civil War the light apparatus was removed from each and stored at Fortress Monroe. The 1864 *Annual Report* stated that "Upon movement of the Army of the Potomac to the south side of the James River, necessitating the use of the highway as a medium for transporting stores and supplies, the lights at Point of Shoals, White Shoals, and Deep Water Shoals were re-established." None of the three survives today.

## Deep Water Shoals Light Station (1868)

Established in 1855, Deep Water Shoals Light in Virginia, on the north side of the James River above Mulberry point, was rebuilt in 1867 using the same hexagonal design that is found at Point of Shoals and White Shoals. The keeper's dwelling and lantern were painted white, while the roof and iron pilings supporting the structure were painted red. (1885 photo by Major Jared A. Smith courtesy of the USCG Historian's Office)

THE U.S. LIGHT-HOUSE BOARD ACHIEVES ITS GOALS

Point of Shoals Light Station

White Shoal Light Station

## Point of Shoals Light Station (1871)

The first screwpile lighthouse on Point of Shoals in the James River in Virginia, just below Mulberry Island point, was constructed in 1855. A new lens fitted with Funck lamps was installed in 1869, but the structure was soon badly damaged by ice and no longer safe. A new screwpile, shown at the top of page 197, was built in 1871, with fog-bell machinery installed in 1973. The white dwelling and tower were surmounted by a red roof and underpinned by red screwpiles. (1885 photo by Major Jared A. Smith courtesy of the USCG Historian's Office)

## White Shoal Light Station (1871)

In 1854 a day beacon was constructed on White Shoal in the James River near Newport News, Virginia. It was replaced in 1855 by a screwpile lighthouse. By 1869 the White Shoals Light was "canted to westward about one foot from vertical at the top, and the whole structure in very unsafe condition."[37] A hexagonal screwpile, shown below, was built in 1871 in two feet of water. Like Deep Water Shoals and Point of Shoals Light, the superstructure was painted white, the roof and iron foundation red. A fog bell was rung by hand. By 1898 the lighthouse sat in four feet of water, and the fog bell was rung by machinery. (1885 photo by Major Jared A. Smith courtesy of the USCG Historian's Office)

# Old Field Point Light Station (1868)

Established on Old Field Point on Long Island Sound in 1823, this New York lighthouse was rebuilt in 1868. In 1856 a new lantern to hold a Fresnel lens had been installed. The original dwelling was of roughcast stone and contained five rooms. It may be the building to the left in this photo. The 1868 dwelling is obviously much larger, although still of rough stone. In 1888 a partition was put up in the old dwelling to provide a barn for the keeper. The lighthouse is now used as the town hall for Old Field. (National Archives #26-LG-13-33)

## Santa Cruz Light Station (1869)

The Santa Cruz Light was built to mark the northern entrance to Monterey Bay on the California coast. The first keeper, Adna Hecox, had 10 children. When he died in 1883, his 29-year-old daughter Laura became keeper and held the post until 1917. Her mother and two other members of the family died in the lighthouse; three others were married there. Once the children were all grown up, Laura converted one room of the six-room keeper's house into a museum to house her collection of biological specimens and historical artifacts.

Laura took the *Instructions to Lighthouse Keepers* on neatness very seriously, even whisking visitors with a big feather duster before they entered the lighthouse. The lamps at Santa Cruz Light were among the first to be converted from lard oil to kerosene. (National Archives #26-LG-67-39) The station does not survive.

## Point Arena Light Station (1870)

The Point Arena Light is located on a headland where coasting traffic must alter course to a more northerly direction.[38] This tall masonry tower was lighted with a first-order lens in 1870. A fog signal was added the following year. It served mariners well until the 1906 earthquake damaged

Point Arena Light Station

the tower, the lens, and the keeper's dwelling beyond repair. In 1908 it was replaced by the first reinforced concrete lighthouse in the nation. (Courtesy of the USCG Historian's Office)

## Point Reyes Light Station (1870)[39]

To aid the safe passage of commerce between Oregon and San Francisco, Congress in 1854 appropriated money to build a lighthouse on the very rugged coast of Point Reyes, 35 miles northwest of San Francisco, but disputes over title to the land dragged on for 15 years. In that period over three-quarters of a million dollars in ships and cargo was lost in shipwrecks on Point Reyes.

Point Reyes Light Station

When work began finally in 1870, a three-mile road from a landing at Drakes Bay up over the steep west headland was the first construction. The idea of incorporating the light tower into the keeper's dwelling was abandoned because frequent heavy fog completely obscured the spot. Talented George Davidson of the Pacific Coast survey chose a spot 275 feet below the dwelling site, where sufficient space could be leveled for a 23-foot cast-iron tower, 296 feet above sea level, and a small shed for watching, working, and sleeping. (The prisms around the light to make it flash every five seconds were revolved by a clockwork arrangement with weights that had to be wound up every two hours and twenty minutes.) Ships at sea can still take bearings on the Point Reyes Light, on the lighthouse at Point Bonita 27 ½ miles southeast, on South Farallon Island Light 17 ¾ miles south and east, and on Point Arena Light 67 miles northeast.

A route down the treacherous cliff was blasted and graded to permit a tramway for transporting tools and materials. Violent winds carried away tools and the first roof on the keeper's house. The most difficult tasks of all were construction and maintenance of the fog signal in a small notch hewn out of the face of the steep cliff 100 feet below the tower, with a coal chute to provide fuel for the steam-powered fog signal.

Keeping the Point Reyes Light in the nineteenth century was so demanding—battering winds, implacable fog and darkness, unrelieved isolation, the relentless shrieking fog signal, the 308 steps (sometimes unclimbable because of wind velocity) between the light and the dwelling, the skimpy wages ($600 to $800 a year)—that one or another of the men (a keeper and three assistants) often refused to follow orders or lapsed into depression, claustrophobia, psychosis, and even violence.

The *San Francisco Chronicle* reported in 1887 that

> . . . a late (and now happily deposed) keeper, [was] notorious for his love of the flowing bowl. It is said that he even regaled himself, when out of whisky, with the alcohol furnished for cleaning lamps, and a familiar sight to the [nearby] ranchman was this genial gentleman lying dead drunk by the roadside, while his horse, attached to the lighthouse wagon, grazed at will over the country.

(Opposite image of tower soon after construction is by Eadweard Muybridge, courtesy of the USCG Historian's Office and the view from a distance on page 201, also probably taken by Muybridge, National Archives #26-LG-66-56)

Point Reyes Light Station

# Cape Hatteras Light Station (1870)

A 90-foot sandstone tower was constructed in 1803 to mark the hazardous Diamond Shoals in an area along the Outer Banks of North Carolina referred to as the "Graveyard of the Atlantic." Mariners made numerous complaints about the effectiveness of the light. Capt. David Porter, commander of the U.S. mail steamer *Georgia*, remarked in 1851,

> Hatteras light, the most important on our coast, and, without doubt the <u>worst</u> [*sic*] light in the world. Cape Hatteras is that point made by all vessels going to the south, and also coming from that direction; the current of the Gulf stream runs so close to the outer point of the shoals that vessels double as close round the breakers as possible, to avoid its influence. . . .[40]

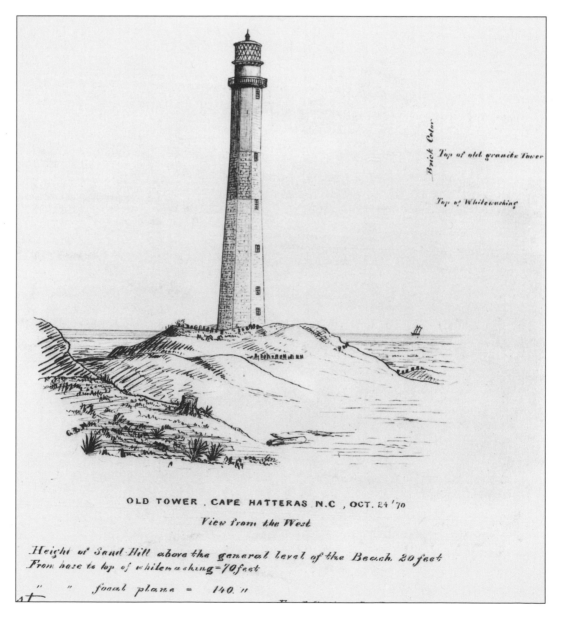

OLD TOWER, CAPE HATTERAS N.C , OCT. 24 '70

*View from the West*

*Height of Sand Hill above the general level of the Beach 20 feet*
*From base to top of whitewashing = 70 feet*
*" " focal plane = 140. "*

THE U.S. LIGHT-HOUSE BOARD ACHIEVES ITS GOALS

In 1854, the tower was heightened with a brick addition to provide a focal height 140 feet above sea level as reflected in the 1870 sketch on the opposite page (National Archives, RG 26).

A new tower was completed in 1870 using 1,250,000 bricks on a granite foundation. Rising over 198 feet above ground level, Cape Hatteras is the tallest lighthouse tower in the United States. The photo above shows the station in the 1890s. The dwelling on the left was built in 1871 to serve as the principal keeper's residence; the duplex on the right, built in 1854, housed two assistants and was later modified to accommodate three assistant keepers. (Ca. 1890s photo by Herbert Bamber, National Archives #26-LG-22-82B)

Because of the threat of shoreline erosion, in 1999 the National Park Service moved the entire station 2,900 feet to the southwest, placing it 1,600 feet from the shoreline, with the same orientation to the sea that it had when it was built. Designated a National Historic Landmark in 1998, the tower is an extremely popular tourist destination in the Cape Hatteras National Seashore.

## Mission Point Light Station (1870)

Located on a point of land dividing Grand Traverse Bay, the Mission Point Light Station was completed on Lake Michigan in 1870 north of Traverse City, Michigan. In 1889 a bulkhead 200 feet long, 4 feet high, and filled with stone was built to protect the frame dwelling. A brick oil house was added in 1898. This lighthouse is still extant. (National Archives #26-LG-56-97)

## Portage River Light Station (1870)

Located in Michigan at the entrance of the Portage River into Lake Superior, the Portage River Light Station guided mariners to the twin cities of Houghton and Hancock, in the heart of copper country. Established in 1856, the original rubblestone station was so damp that interior wood floors and fittings rotted. It was replaced in 1870 with the brick tower and attached keeper's dwelling shown at the top opposite. (Ca. 1890s photo by Herbert Bamber, National Archives #26-LG-52-38) This station's function was replaced with the Keweenaw Pier Lights. The keeper's dwelling is now a private residence.

THE U.S. LIGHT-HOUSE BOARD ACHIEVES ITS GOALS

Portage River Light Station

## Sisters Island Light Station (1870)

This limestone lighthouse in New York State was constructed in 1870, after a nine-year negotiation to obtain title to the land. It marked a difficult channel on the Canadian side of Three Sisters Island in the St. Lawrence River. The square 60-foot tower contained a sixth-order lens and

was attached to the rear of the two-and-one-half-story keeper's dwelling. The framing supports on the gables are in the Stick Style popular at the time. Two dormer windows on the front and deep window seats in the large rooms make this a very comfortable dwelling. Keepers had to keep a constant watch on the light when the shad flies were swarming, because they occasionally were numerous enough to block the oxygen intake and extinguish the flame in the lamps.[41] Deactivated in the 1950s, the station is now privately owned. (National Archives #26-LG-47-29)

Halfway Rock Light Station

THE U.S. LIGHT-HOUSE BOARD ACHIEVES ITS GOALS

# Halfway Rock Light Station (1871)

The handsome granite tower opposite stands on Halfway Rock in Casco Bay midway between Cape Small Point and Cape Elizabeth and lies off Bailey Island in the arc of the outer approaches to the harbor at Portland, Maine. "The site is isolated, and consequently the landing of materials and the employment of laborers were necessarily more than ordinarily difficult and expensive."[42] The tower was completed and lit in 1871 and a boat-slip and masonry boathouse added the following year. In 1888 "a pyramidal skeleton bell-tower, 43 feet high, was built [southwest of the tower] of yellow pine timbers 10 inches square, heavily bolted to the ledge," and a 1,000-pound bell with striking machine was put in place.[43] In 1889 "a boat-house 18 feet by 24 feet in plan, of yellow pine securely bolted both to the ledge and to the tower [on the west side], was built with two dwelling-rooms in the loft."[44] (National Archives #26-LG-1-62B) The station survives as an active aid to navigation.

# Bodie Island Light Station (1872)

A light station on Bodie Island south of Oregon Inlet in North Carolina was established in 1848. A storm that year cut the inlet through the Outer Banks. A new tower was constructed in 1859 with a third-order lens. The lens was removed in 1862 during the Civil War. The 1867 *Annual Report* states that "This lighthouse was totally destroyed by the rebels during the war. . . ."

In 1871-72 five shipwrecks off the coast were valued at more than the cost of a new lighthouse. In 1872 a new tower, shown on page 210, was built four miles north of Oregon Inlet and fitted with a first-order lens. Birds flew into the lantern in 1873, seriously damaging the lens. Heavy wire netting was rigged around the lantern to deflect future damage.[45] (Ca. 1890s photo by Herbert Bamber, National Archives #26-LG-71-63)

Today the station continues as an active aid to navigation in the Cape Hatteras National Seashore; the keepers' dwelling houses a small museum and bookstore.

Bodie Island Light Station

---

## Bullock Point Light Station (1872)

This light station in the Providence River, Rhode Island, was constructed in 1872 on a shoal off Bullock Point on the east side of the channel. In 1875 the cut stone foundation was enlarged and the frame dwelling added. "In December and January the work was much delayed by the severity of the weather and running ice."[46] In 1889, 1894, and 1898 between 200 and 300 tons of riprap was placed around the pier. An oil house was added in 1900. (Opposite photo courtesy of the Society for the Preservation of New England Antiquities) Severely damaged in the 1938 hurricane, the station does not survive.

# St. Simons Island Light Station (1872)

A light station existed from 1811 on the south end of St. Simons Island at the entrance to Simons Sound on the coast of Georgia. Congress established a naval station in nearby Brunswick in 1857, increasing the importance of the St. Simons Island Light. The tower was blown up during the Civil War. Work to replace it after the war ended was held up when malaria killed the contractor and felled his workmen.[47] The photo below shows the construction of the keeper's dwelling and the base of the tower. (National Archives #26-LG-29-20)

Shown opposite, the 100-foot tower, completed in 1872, held a third-order lens. (National Archives #26-LG-29-21) The 1874 *Annual Report* stated that "this station is very unhealthy, and it is attributed to the stagnant water in several ponds in the vicinity which have no outlet." The ponds were drained the following year and again in 1884. In 1887 an earthquake damaged some light panels, and the dwelling was struck by lightning the same year. Modern lightning conductors were placed on the building. A fireproof brick oil house was added in 1891. In 1895 a range beacon was hung in a small triangular structure to the front of the lighthouse to guide small vessels over the bar. The original lens is still in operation as an active aid to navigation while the dwelling houses a museum.

THE U.S. LIGHT-HOUSE BOARD ACHIEVES ITS GOALS

St. Simons Light Station

# South Manitou Island Light Station (1872)

A light station was established on South Manitou Island in Lake Michigan in 1839. The entire station was rebuilt in 1858. By 1867 the buildings required extensive repairs. The Light-House Board felt the station should be improved because "the principal commerce of the lake" passes between the island and the mainland. "It is also a guide to a harbor of refuge, which is probably used more than any other on the entire chain of lakes."[48] The improvements made in 1870 included a much taller (104 feet) brick tower holding a third-order lens, connected by a long passageway to the 1858 brick dwelling. A steam fog signal was added in 1875, replacing the fog bell.

South Manitou Island Light Station

South Manitou Island Station was deactivated in 1958 and is part of Sleeping Bear Dunes National Seashore. (National Archives #26-LG-56-93)

## Sullivans Island Range Light Station (1872)

The light station on Sullivans Island in South Carolina was established in 1848 to guide ships over the Charleston Bar and into Charleston Harbor. In 1859 Congressman William Miles suggested to Secretary of the Treasury Howell Cobb that the keeper at Sullivans Island have his salary increased because he was tending two lights. The Secretary replied that "the fact of there being two beacons at a light station has never influenced in fixing salaries, as the keeping of two small lights of this description are generally less onerous than the keeping of a larger single light."[49]

The station was destroyed in 1861. Immediately after the surrender of Charleston in 1865, a temporary beacon was placed in a frame skeleton tower atop the roof of a private house on Sullivans Island to mark the channel to where the wreck of the monitor *Weehawken* lay. A light vessel was placed over the wreck. Negotiations for the purchase of land delayed the establishment of permanent range lights until 1872, when they were placed on government land at Fort Moultrie. "The front beacon is a frame structure resting on the parapet of the fort. The rear one is an open-frame square pyramid. The keeper's dwelling is detached. . . . [When they were lighted] on July 15, the light on the light-ship was discontinued. . . ."[50] (Bottom photo of keeper's dwelling by Herbert Bamber, ca. 1890s, National Archives #LG-30-13)

> The lights of the Sullivan Island range are red. Besides marking the range from Pumpkin Hill Bar, they mark a good range over the Southwest Bar, so that vessels coming up from southerly ports can enter Charleston Harbor at night, without the necessity of going up to the main ship-channel, thereby saving a run of several miles.[51]

In 1878 the front beacon of the range was moved from the parapet to the glacis of Fort Moultrie, set upon brick piers, and enclosed in a picket fence. The following year it was raised six feet and placed upon a brick basement, which was fitted up as an oil room. In 1883, it was painted red,

as shown in the 1885 photo below (National Archives #26-LG-30-12). In 1886, because of changes in the channel, the front beacon was removed from its brick substructure, moved 12 feet to the west, and put on a wooden tramway. A number of other adjustments were made in the years after 1885, until in 1899 the rear range was discontinued in favor of two front ranges. The station no longer exists.

Sullivans Island Front Range

# Craighill Channel Lower Range Light Station (1873)

The Craighill Channel Lower Range Lights define the Craighill Channel, northern Chesapeake Bay, in Maryland. The Light-House Board wanted a strong foundation for the rear range to withstand ice pile-ups in the winter. A cofferdam of sheet piling was built around the entire site; piles were driven and cut off evenly, then a grillage of timbers placed on top, and finally the nine piers of Port Deposit granite were constructed. The

THE U.S. LIGHT-HOUSE BOARD ACHIEVES ITS GOALS

cofferdam was then dismantled. Upon this foundation was anchored an open-frame pyramidal structure with a central square column surrounded by a keeper's dwelling at the bottom as shown in photo below. (1885 photo by Major Jared A. Smith courtesy of The Mariners' Museum, Newport News, Virginia) The column contained a stairway to the lantern, which held a fourth-order range lens.[52]

The front range, completed in 1874, was located 2.4 miles south of the rear range. The one-and-a-half-story cast-iron-plate, brick-lined tower sat on a cast-iron cylinder attached to a wooden caisson, one of the earliest caisson lighthouse foundations built. The keeper's dwelling was removed from the rear range after the light was automated; both lights continue as active aids to navigation.

# Fort Tompkins Light Station (1873)

A light station was established in 1828 on a bluff near Fort Tompkins on Staten Island, New York. The black lantern on the tower on the white dwelling with Mansard roof received a fourth-order lens in 1855. In 1863 artillery practice at Fort Tompkins seriously damaged the lantern glass, requiring refitting. In 1871 the lighthouse had to be moved to make room for an artillery battery. The light was placed temporarily on a wooden frame until a new tower could be built and lighted (1873).

The 1892 *Annual Report* stated that

> The light at Fort Tompkins is well back of the point it was intended to mark. It is therefore proposed to move it from there to an angle of the stone fort at Fort Wadsworth, where it will better serve as a mark to the channel leading directly into New York Harbor. A fog signal at Fort Wadsworth would be of especial service to the large commerce going through the Narrows during thick weather. The fog bell at Fort Lafayette is serviceable to vessels bound to Coney Island, but is too distant to be of much use to vessels using the other and more frequented side of the channel.

In 1895 the *Annual Report* said that "a battery for five high-power modern rifles is to be completed in the rear of the lighthouse. This fact makes it more important than before that this light should be moved." In 1903 the Fort Tompkins Light was replaced by the Fort Wadsworth Light. The old tower no longer survives. (National Archives #26-LG-11-69)

## Daufuskie Island Range Light Station (1873)

The range lights shown here were built in 1873 on Daufuskie Island to facilitate passage through shoals and currents of the inside passage from Port Royal Harbor to the Savannah River in South Carolina. The bay is open and exposed to the Atlantic, the channel not more than six and one-half feet deep, with a very irregular bottom. The front beacon was on an open frame structure with a steamer lens (see photo above). The rear range was a dioptric fifth-order lens atop a tower on one end of the keeper's dwelling (see photo on facing page). The two were 750 yards apart.

A boat landing and boathouse were added in 1875. The hurricane of 1883 severely damaged the station, requiring extensive repairs. Further damage in an earthquake led to structural repairs. Outbuildings were rebuilt in 1889,

THE U.S. LIGHT-HOUSE BOARD ACHIEVES ITS GOALS

a fireproof oil house added in 1892, and a large cistern in 1895. The station no longer exists. (Photos of both front and rear ranges taken in 1885 by Major Jared A. Smith, courtesy of the USCG Historian's Office)

## Mare Island Light Station (1873)

A naval base was constructed on Mare Island in San Pablo Bay in the 1850s. To facilitate navigation up the Napa River, a lighthouse was located on the southern end of the island in 1873. Its two keepers were both women, first a Mrs. Watson, and then Kate McDougal, whose Lighthouse Inspector husband drowned while delivering payrolls to lighthouse keepers.

The light station was perched high on a cliff and was reached by a long flight of stairs. Supplies delivered by tenders every three or four months were winched up the cliff in a wheeled cart on rails located to the left of the stairs. Water also came by tender until a rain catch basin was constructed in 1890. A fog bell at the end of the pier was activated by the keeper when fog crept across the bay.

Kate McDougal and her daughters kept the light from 1881 until 1916, when the Mare Island Light was made superfluous by the new Carquinez Strait Light on the Vallejo shore. The station no longer exists. (National Archives #26-LG-64-68)

# Bluff Point (Valcour Island) Light Station (1874)

A lighthouse was built on Valcour Island in Lake Champlain in 1874, after several years of negotiations with the owner of the chosen site. He wanted to build a wharf nearby and have permission to cross the lighthouse grounds. This was agreed to inasmuch as supplies would have to be landed and transported from the wharf to the lighthouse. The blue limestone building still stands on a high bluff on the island, which is located on the New York State side of the lake.

This photo shows a woman by the door, probably Mary Herwerth, who assisted her husband, a Civil War veteran, in keeping the light until his death in 1881, when she was appointed to succeed him. She continued her duties until 1902. (National Archives #26-LG-11-20)

# Spectacle Reef Light Station (1874)

In justifying a request for an appropriation to build a lighthouse on Spectacle Reef, a dangerous shoal at the northern end of Lake Huron in Michigan, the Board indicated that it "is in the way of all vessels beating through Lake Huron, and is probably more dreaded by navigation than any other danger now unmarked throughout the entire chain of lakes . . ." They estimated it would take $316,093.20 to build, a sum less than the value of two ships that were wrecked on the shoal in the autumn of 1867.

The design had to consider heavy wave action—"the seas have a fetch of about one hundred and seventy miles"[53]—and the ice fields, thousands of acres in area and often two feet thick, moved by strong currents. The construction was overseen by Major O.M. Poe, who had served as General Sherman's chief engineer during his march to the sea. It took 20 months to build over a period of four years. Supplies were transported from a depot at Scammon's Harbor, 16 miles away. In 11 feet of water, a "pier of protection" was erected to provide a "still pond" 48 feet square in which a temporary cofferdam was placed as well as a landing stage for materials and a foundation for temporary quarters for the workmen.[54] To form the crib foundation, two-foot stones were cut to lock together in courses. The courses were fastened together using wrought-iron bolts. "For 34 feet up the tower is solid, from thence it is hollow, and in it are 5 rooms one above the other, each 14 feet in diameter . . . The walls of the hollow portion are 5 feet 6 inches at the bottom, and taper to 18 inches . . . The interior is lined with a 4-inch brick wall, between which and the masonry is a 2-inch air space."[55]

Completed in 1874, the lighthouse cost $375,000. Its durability was soon tested; in 1875, the ice was piled up to a height of 30 feet around the lighthouse when the keepers returned at the start of shipping season. They had to cut a passageway to the door. Automated in 1982, Spectacle Reef continues as an active aid to navigation. (Photo courtesy of The Mariners' Museum, Newport News, Virginia)

## Point Fermin Light Station (1874)

The lighthouse at the entrance to San Pedro Harbor on the California is built on a similar plan to Mare Island and East Brother Lighthouses in California and Hereford Inlet Lighthouse in New Jersey. The design is attributed to Paul J. Pelz, designer of the Library of Congress. The lantern panes and fourth-order Fresnel lens were shipped from France by way of Cape Horn. Mary Smith obtained the first keeper's position, transferring from the Ediz Hook Light Station, Washington. Her sister, Helen, served as her assistant. During World War II the lantern room was removed and replaced by a radar lookout. (Ca. 1890s photo by Herbert Bamber courtesy of the USCG Historian's Office)

Point Fermin Light Station

## Thomas Point Shoal Light Station (1875)

The screwpile structure on Thomas Point Shoal replaced an onshore station established at the entrance of the South River, Maryland, in 1820 and rebuilt in 1840. Vessels in the main channel of the Chesapeake Bay often could not see the shore light marking the shoal. By the 1870s, most exposed sites likely to get ice buildup during the winter were using caisson-type lighthouses. Budget constraints made the Light-House Board opt for

THE U.S. LIGHT-HOUSE BOARD ACHIEVES ITS GOALS

a cheaper screwpile structure at Thomas Point. When completed in 1875, the six-room hexagonal building supported an eight-sided fourth-order lantern containing a third-and-a-half-order lens. Rain water was collected in four iron tanks, each with a capacity of 200 gallons.[56] Automated in 1986, Thomas Point was the last manned lighthouse on the Chesapeake. As the last intact, cottage-type, screwpile lighthouse "in situ" in the United States, Thomas Point Shoal Light Station was made a National Historic Landmark in 1999. Note the ice breaker on the right side of the photo below. (1885 photo by Major Jared A. Smith, National Archives #26-LG-25-54)

Thomas Point Shoal Light Station

# Block Island Southeast Light Station (1875)

The Block Island Southeast Light Station constructed in 1874 on an island off the coast of Rhode Island was intended to be a showpiece. Its high-style Victorian Gothic design is a departure from the utilitarian plans generally used. Some speculate that the Light-House Board felt that since Block Island was a popular summer resort, the lighthouse would serve as a highly visible representative of the Board and federal government.

Moved back from eroding cliffs in 1993, Block Island Southeast Light Station, a National Historic Landmark, continues as an active aid to navigation and popular tourist destination. (Courtesy of the USCG Historian's Office)

## Tue Marshes Light Station (1875)

This square screwpile lighthouse was completed in 1875 on a shoal about one-half mile north of Tue Point at the entrance to the York River in Virginia. The white keeper's dwelling was surmounted by a lantern containing a fifth-order lens. The fog bell was struck by machinery, alternating a single and a double blow. The house is gone; the screwpile foundation now supports a modern optic. (1885 photo by Major Jared A. Smith courtesy of the USCG Historian's Office)

# Thirty Mile Point Light Station (1876)

A light was recommended by the Light-House Board at a point thirty miles from the mouth of the Niagara River on Lake Ontario in 1872. An 1873 architectural rendering shows a far more ornate structure than the one shown in the plans approved by the Light-house Board in 1874. (National Archives, RG 26) The limestone tower and dwelling were completed in early 1876.

During the second half of the century, the number of stations with assistant keepers increased significantly under the Light-House Board. Since these families were required to both work and live in close proximity, it is not surprising that disputes did occur. In 1883, F. W. Vaugh, an employee of the Pension Office in Washington, wrote on behalf of his brother Hiram, an assistant keeper at Thirty Mile Point,

> . . . there has existed for some time trouble between the families of a domestic nature for which my brother & his family are not responsible either for its origin or continuance. My brother writes me that the Inspector has just made them a visit & informed him that it must be settled before he gets back to Buffalo or he, my brother, will be discharged. . . . My brother is a crippled Union soldier & the Principal was not in the army, and this request is made that injustice may not de done him my brother & his family.[57]

Deactivated in 1959, the station is now part of Golden Hill State Park.

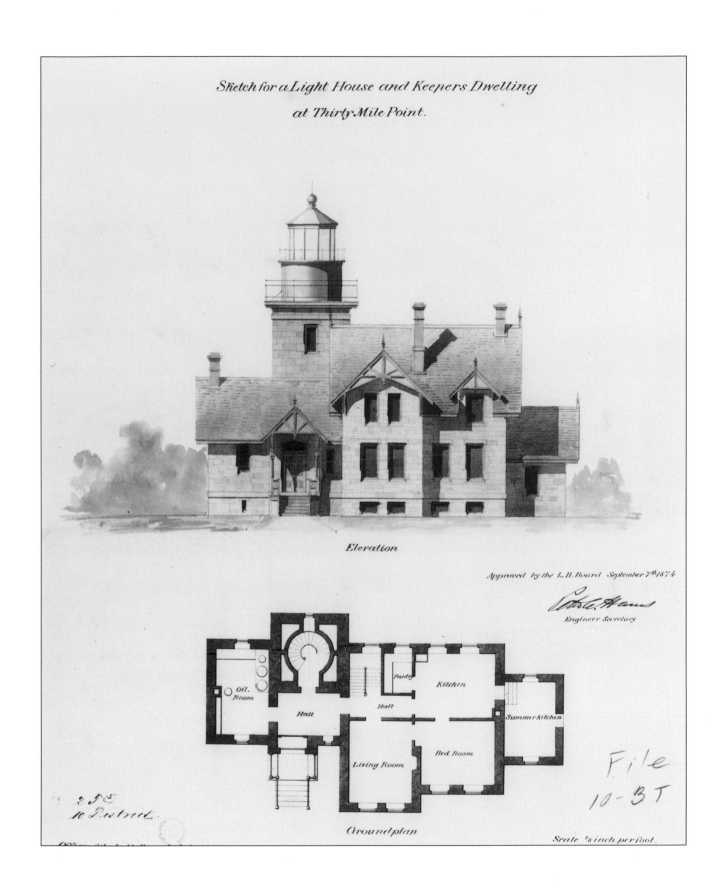

Sketch for a Light House and Keepers Dwelling
at Thirty Mile Point.

Elevation

Approved by the L.H.Board September 7th 1874

*Engineer Secretary*

Oil. Room

Hall

Hall

Pantry

Kitchen

Summer Kitchen

Living Room

Bed Room

File
10-BT

2 5
10 District.

Ground plan

Scale ⅛ inch per foot.

## Morris Island Light Station (1876)

The light station on Morris Island at the entrance to Charleston Harbor in South Carolina was established in 1767. An 1827 report by the keeper listed 10 lamps in the lantern, two of which are "in very bad order . . . [and] . . . totally unfit for service."[58] The 1849 *Light List* mentioned a 102-foot tower. A first-order lens was installed in 1857.

Confederate troops during the Civil War destroyed the lantern and lens and demolished the tower.[59] The site selected for its rebuilding after the War permitted the Morris Island Light to be the rear range for the two Pumpkin-Hill Channel beacon lights completed in 1870. The tower was built on a pile and grillage foundation, with outer rows of piles driven 50 feet into sand and mud. The tower base below ground was of concrete or rubble masonry, on which rested the 150-foot brick shaft. The unhealthiness of the locality prevented work during summer months. The tower was completed in 1876 and a first-order lens installed. The keeper's

THE U.S. LIGHT-HOUSE BOARD ACHIEVES ITS GOALS

dwelling was completed the following year.[60] (National Archives #26-LG-27-5)

The front range was dislodged in an 1879 storm, moved back 200 feet, and placed upon a brick foundation. The front range, pictured above in 1885, was moved 180 feet south of its original position to serve as the range for the South Channel until 1899. (Photo by Major Jared A. Smith, National Archives #26-LG-28-36)

In 1888 the Pumpkin-Hill Channel range was moved 180 feet south and the rear beacon discontinued, replaced by a post light. Erosion led to further moves of the beacons, until they were abandoned in 1899. Further erosion led to the establishment of the new Texas Tower for the Charleston Light in 1962. The tower, unused in 1999, still stands, surrounded by water; the keeper's dwelling was destroyed in a 1938 hurricane.

---

## Stratford Shoal Light Station (1877)

Lightship *No. 15* was stationed between 1837 and 1877 in Long Island Sound in Connecticut on Middle Ground, midway between Stratford Point and Old Field Point. It was replaced in 1877 by the light station shown on next page. (National Archives #26-LG-17-18) The gray octagonal tower projects from the south side of the square house. The beginning of construction of the pier on which it is built is shown in the second photo. (National Archives #26-LG-17-16) This station is still an active aid to navigation.

Stratford Shoal Light Station

THE U.S. LIGHT-HOUSE BOARD ACHIEVES ITS GOALS

# Fowey Rocks Light Station (1878)

Named for the wreck of the British warship HMS *Fowey*, which sunk there in 1748, Fowey Rocks was located at the extreme northern point of the Florida Keys. The Fowey Rocks Lighthouse was the fifth offshore diskpile structure built along the keys. Divers began construction by leveling a portion of the reef five feet below the surface at low tide. Next iron disks were positioned to receive the pilings, which were driven 11 feet into the coral. The first deck was completed in summer 1876 before bad weather hindered progress until the following March. Two vessels ran aground on the reef while work was in progress. The two-story iron-sheeted octagonal keeper's dwelling had eight rooms with wooden interior walls. It was painted white with green trim and shutters. An iron cylinder enclosed the stairs leading to the watch room and lantern. The first-order Fresnel lens was lit for the first time on June 15, 1878; an automatic modern optic is used today.[61] (National Archives #26-LG-69-56)

American Shoal Light Station

THE U.S. LIGHT-HOUSE BOARD ACHIEVES ITS GOALS

## American Shoal Light Station (1880)

Using the same design as Fowey Rocks, American Shoal Lighthouse was the last of its type constructed along the Florida Keys. A day beacon was placed on the shoal in 1850, but was of little value to night navigation. After repeated requests, Congress appropriated $75,000 in 1878. A New Jersey firm secured the contract for the ironwork for $47,000. As with all other reef lights, the company assembled the structure before shipment to ensure a perfect fit. Construction proceeded in the same manner as with Fowey Rocks except without the weather hazards. The towers were identical except in colors and light characteristics used to distinguish them. The keeper's dwelling at American Shoal was painted brown; the first-order light was flashing. An additional $50,000 was required to complete the station, which was first lit in 1880.[62] Now within a marine sanctuary, American Shoal Light continues as an active aid to navigation. (National Archives #26-LG-31-5A)

## Cape Henry Light Station (1881)

The first tower at Cape Henry was completed in 1792 as the first federal public works project, nearly 80 years after Virginia Colony's Governor Spotswood first proposed the project. Designed and built by John McComb, Jr., the sandstone tower marked the south side of the entrance to the Chesapeake Bay in Virginia. One of the station's early keepers, T. Burroughs, sent the following request to the Norfolk collector in 1817:

> I have to solicit you for a horse. I have bean [*sic*] allowed one by the Secretary some years ago and that having died leaves me without one, the use of the horse is to cart wood for fires & brush to put around the dwelling, which collects sand to the foundation, a cart would also be usefull as the brush & wood can't be moved without one.[63]

In 1872, inspectors reported cracks extending from the base to nearly the top of the tower on the north and south walls. The Light-House Board recommended that a new and more substantial lighthouse be built since this was considered "one of the first lights of importance along the coast." The foundation of the new tower was made of seven parts cut granite, three parts very coarse sand and gravel, and one part imperial German Portland cement. Cast-iron-plate sections were "neatly fitted and correctly marked" and assembled in place on September 15, 1881. The interior lining, stair landings, and brackets were completed on November 15. The first-order lens was tested and the lighthouse was turned over to the keeper on

Cape Henry Light Station

THE U.S. LIGHT-HOUSE BOARD ACHIEVES ITS GOALS

December 15, 1881.[64] Reaching a height of 163 feet, the new Cape Henry tower became and still remains the tallest cast-iron-plate lighthouse in the United States. Opposite photo shows the 1881 construction of second tower with first tower in the background. (Courtesy of The Mariners' Museum, Newport News, Virginia)

## Rock Island Light Station (1882)

The Rock Island Light Station, one of six lighthouses on the St. Lawrence River in New York State, was established in 1848 where the St. Lawrence River flows into Lake Ontario. Only the fieldstone smokehouse remains from this earlier period. The iron tower shown here, lined with brick and wood, was built in 1882 to replace the wooden lantern on the keeper's dwelling. It held a sixth-order lens and was built on a concrete foundation a few feet from the island, connected by a stone and concrete walkway to the two-story shingle dwelling,[69] which was rebuilt in 1885 on the old foundation and using the material of the old dwelling as far as possible. A well was sunk through granite, and water obtained at a depth of 36 feet. In 1895 the tower was raised five feet so that it could be seen over the roof of the dwelling, with a solid octagonal wall of red granite laid in Portland cement mortar underneath. A generator was installed in 1900 to pump water from the river for domestic use and in case of fire. The station is now part of Thousand Islands State Park. (National Archives #26-LG-47-4)

# Point Conception Light Station (1882)

The light station at Point Conception at the west entrance to the Santa Barbara Channel on the California coast was established in 1855. The light was provided by a first-order lens; a steam fog signal was installed in 1872, using "an abundant supply of water from an adjoining spring."[65]

An earthquake in 1868 damaged the dwelling to the point that iron rods were used to reinforce it.[66] By 1875 the Light-House Board reported the dwelling as being in bad condition. In 1880 Congress was asked for $38,000 to rebuild the tower and other structures, plus $10,000

> with which to secure title to the land on which the station is located. . . . This station is one of the oldest established on this coast, and is also one of the most important. All sailing-vessels and steamers change course when off this point, either in going up or down the coast, and the extinguishment of the light and stoppages of the fog signal would make navigation on this part of the coast extremely hazardous.[67]

Funds were appropriated in 1881, and "the materials purchased, shipped, and safely landed through the surf at El Coxo [Landing]," then hauled up to the site. An extra set of machinery and whistles used at Point Reyes was used temporarily until the new fog signal building was completed and the signal installed. A coal chute was built from the top of the bluff down to the fog signal building. The brick keeper's dwelling was repaired and expanded to accommodate two families. An old cottage was repaired; a new cottage, a storehouse, and a coal shed were added—all of them visible in the second photo.[68]

Point Conception continues as an active aid to navigation with its first-order lens and original clockwork intact. (1894 photos by Herbert Bamber courtesy of the USCG Historian's Office)

# Fort Point Light Station (1882)

Ceded by Texas to the United States in 1845, "the land known as Fort Point comprised 15 acres and was situated on the east end of Galveston Island." Because the "north end of Galveston Island had shifted to westward," there was some question by 1879 as to what exactly was federal property. Pilots and others concerned with navigation of Galveston Bay wanted "a light at, on, or as near as possible to, the northern end of the pile breakwater, so that a vessel entering the harbor at night or in thick weather would keep clear of this structure and also of the shoal close to and due East of this proposed site."[70] Unfortunately, the breakwater was disintegrating and the sand shifted with every gale. The best location was about 1,000 feet northeast of the northern end of the breakwater, near the channel edge of the shoal, where the bottom was hard and stable. Since the site was underwater, ownership was not a problem. The white, hexagonal, iron pile lighthouse was completed and lit in 1882, with a fourth-order light.[71] Fort Point Light was downgraded to a fog signal station in 1909, then demolished in the 1950s. (National Archives #26-LG-36-5)

## Belle Isle Light Station (1882)

The 1877 *Annual Report* recommended that

> a light be established at the northern point of Belle Isle to guide vessels
> into the south channel of the Detroit River, which is almost exclusively
> used. The reefs extending out from Isle aux Peche and Belle Isle make it
> difficult to strike this channel in dark nights, and a large number of
> vessels annually grounded on one or the other of these reefs.

This Michigan lighthouse was completed and lit in 1882. The keeper's
dwelling, boathouse, and a stone retaining wall with an iron railing around
the site were completed the following year. The circular oil house to the left
of the dwelling was added in 1891, the year this photo was taken.
(National Archives #26-LG-49-68B)

The light station was part of the St. Clair Lifeboat Station until it was
replaced by a modern Coast Guard Station.

## Ram Island Light Station (1883)

Located at the entrance to Boothbay Harbor on the coast of Maine, Ram Island Light Station was established in 1883. "The tower is of granite from the base, twenty feet upward and of brick above that; the granite is gray,—the brick, red,—the lantern iron, painted black. The tower is connected with the shore by a bridge [on iron pilings], and the keeper's dwelling is a frame house painted white with red roof, 280 feet SE. from the tower."[72] A boathouse and fuel house were built as well. In 1897 a 1,000-pound bell, struck by machinery, was added. (Courtesy of the USCG Historian's Office)

# Point Robinson Light Station (1885)

Located on the northeast end of Maury Island in Puget Sound (Washington State), the Point Robinson Station was established as a fog signal station in 1885. The boiler and the fog signal machinery were formerly in use at Point Adams. The tender *Shubrick* delivered these and other needed materials. The one-story frame fog signal building was the first structure built. The keeper's dwelling, a story-and-a-half frame dwelling, is in the background. High water soon washed logs against the dwelling fence, prompting construction of a 400-foot log bulkhead around the spit. The lantern on a temporary skeleton tower shown here was added in 1887. (Ca. 1890s photo by Herbert Bamber, National Archives #26-LG-62-48) In 1894, 1895, and 1896 hundreds of cubic yards of stone were placed in front of the bulkhead. This photo shows clearly the damage done by high seas. A new tower for the lens lantern was installed in 1897. An entirely new lighthouse and fog signal were built here in 1915.

## Ship Island Light Station (1886)

Ship Island lies off the Mississippi Gulf Coast, and is seven miles long and half a mile wide. The light station built there in 1853 to guide ships to an anchorage on the island had a conical brick tower 45 feet tall and a one-story brick keeper's dwelling close by. The specifications issued by the Superintendent of Lights included "an outhouse, five feet by four, to be shingled and painted; [and] a well sufficiently deep to procure good water at a convenient distance from the dwelling house, to be bricked and furnished with curb, iron chain, windlass and strong bucket."

By 1886 the tower was considered no longer safe. A new, square, wooden tower was erected 300 feet away and the pedestal and lens transferred from the old tower. A fourth-order lens was moved there from Barnegat Light. The old tower was taken down and the bricks placed around the piers of the new dwelling and tower to hold the sand in place. (Courtesy of the USCG Historian's Office.)

The dwelling was destroyed in 1969 by Hurricane Camille, the tower in 1972 by vandals.

# Ponce de Leon Inlet Light Station (1887)

The first tower established in 1835 at Ponce de Leon (Mosquito) Inlet in Florida, was never lit, first because oil had not been ordered to light the lamps, then because a violent storm undermined the tower, and finally because an Indian raiding party further damaged the leaning tower, which was abandoned and left to fall into the sea. After repeated requests, Congress authorized funds for planning a new tower in 1882. The

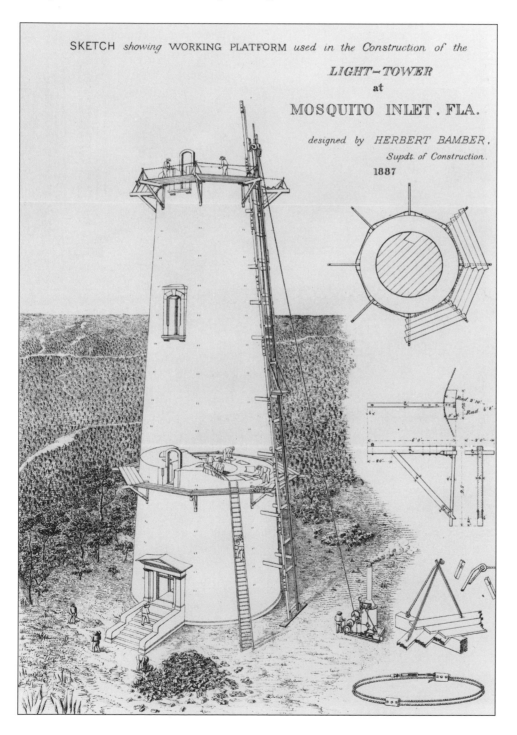

SKETCH *showing* WORKING PLATFORM *used in the Construction of the*
LIGHT-TOWER
at
MOSQUITO INLET. FLA.
*designed by* HERBERT BAMBER,
*Supdt. of Construction.*
1887

The U.S. Light-House Board Achieves Its Goals

construction site was prepared in 1884; a tramway transported the building materials from the wharf as shown in top photo opposite. (National Archives #26-LG-28-50, 1885) The foundation of the tower, shown in bottom photo opposite, was completed in 1885. (National Archives #26-LG-28-43)

As seen in the 1887 construction drawing on page 247, the tower walls are not solid. (National Archives, RG 26) An inner and outer wall are connected by evenly spaced sections of brick similar to the spokes of a wheel. While the outer wall tapers to the lantern, the inner wall retains a constant 12-foot diameter.[73]

The station, including a principal and two assistant keepers' dwellings, oil house, pump house, and three woodshed/privies, was completed and lit in 1887. (National Archives #26-LG-28-54) Still intact and serving as a museum, the station was designated a National Historic Landmark in 1998.

Ponce de Leon Inlet Light Station

*Front Elevation.*

## Horn Island Light Station (1887)

The 1868 *Annual Report* noted that

> the growing importance of Pascagoula River, which penetrates far into
> the rich pine forests bordering the northern shore of the Mississippi
> Sound, the artificial deepening of the bar of the river and the natural
> deepening of the entrance called Horn Island Pass, have induced the
> Board to recommend . . . the erection of a new light-house on Horn
> Island. The ground is very favorable, being hard sand, and more elevated
> than Ship Island.

Horn Island in Mississippi was one of the barrier islands that formed
Mississippi Sound. The first lighthouse, a square wooden dwelling on five
iron piles, was completed in 1874, but shifting sands soon threatened to
undermine the structure. Its keeper for 20 years was Civil War hero Martin
Freeman, who had served as "the pilot guiding Admiral David Farragut's

fleet through the torpedo fields at Mobile Bay. He passed the forts riding the top of the flagship's mainmast as enemy shells whistled past . . . He was seriously wounded when a torpedo he was removing exploded. Freeman's gallantry earned him the Medal of Honor, as well as a job as lighthouse keeper."[74]

A new one-and-a-half-story lighthouse was constructed in 1887 on what was considered the stablest part of the island, with the lantern and fourth-order lens from the earlier structure placed on the roof. A thousand feet of barbed wire had to be erected in 1888 to keep the station from being overrun by cattle. In 1901 the station, again threatened by erosion, was moved and set on 17 foundation piles in about two feet of water. Two cisterns were placed on foundations of eight piles under the dwelling.

A hurricane in 1906 washed away the lighthouse and half of the island, drowning keeper Charles Johnson, his wife, and daughter. Yet a third lighthouse on the same plan was built in 1908 in 21 feet of water alongside the dredged channel. It does not survive. (Drawing from National Archives, RG 26; 1892 image, National Archives #26-LG-36-72)

## Jordan Point Light Station (1887)

The first lighthouse on Jordan Point in the James River near Hopewell, Virginia, was first constructed in 1855, the same year that three screwpile lighthouses were built in the James. The 1873 *Light List* describes a light on the keeper's dwelling. Erosion threatened and was temporarily held in check by a seawall built in 1875. Machinery was installed that year to ring the fog bell. The lighthouse shown here was constructed in 1887. Erosion again threatened, prompting the erection in 1892 of a bulkhead. The station no longer exists. (National Archives #26-LG-23-2)

## Fourteen Foot Bank Light Station (1888)

The Fourteen Foot Bank lighthouse, which replaced Lightship *No. 19* (1876-1888), stands in Delaware Bay near Bowers Beach in Delaware. America's first pneumatic caisson lighthouse structure, it is built on a 73-foot-high cylindrical foundation that expands at the top under the main gallery. The two-story dwelling, painted brown, has a gable roof surmounted by the lantern, which rises from the east side of the dwelling. This light is still an active aid to navigation. (National Archives #26-LG-20-27)

# Ballast Point Light Station (1890)

The discussion of a light at Ballast Point to guide ships into San Diego Harbor began in 1883. Congress appropriated $25,000 in 1889, and the construction of the Stick-style lighthouse was completed in 1890 using the same design as two other California lighthouses at San Luis Obispo (1890) and Table Bluff (1892). The iron-work for the lantern was done in San Francisco and assembled on top of the dwelling. A fifth-order lens was installed. A fog-bell house was built at the same time and the bell and clockwork for striking the bell were put in place. (The bell is now on display in the San Diego Maritime Museum.) Water was collected in wooden tanks with roofs to prevent evaporation.

The assistant keeper's house to the right was occupied by the assistant keeper, who with the principal keeper tended the lighted buoys in the harbor using the station's launch. In 1900 there were 12 lighted buoys in the Bay and a few at the entrance. Ballast Point Light Station was razed in 1961 to make way for an expansion of the nearby submarine base.[75] (1893 photo by Herbert Bamber courtesy of the USCG Historian's Office)

THE U.S. LIGHT-HOUSE BOARD ACHIEVES ITS GOALS

## Devils Island Light Station (1891)

The Devils Island Light was established in Wisconsin on the most northern of the Apostle Islands in Lake Superior in 1891. "Devils Island is an isolated station with no adequate harbor. The light, which is flashing and of the third order, will become one of the most important turning points in Lake Superior. In addition it is to have a fog signal, and provision must be made, therefore, for not less than three keepers."[76] Because funds appropriated in 1888 were inadequate, a temporary tower was erected in 1891, described as

> a square pyramidal skeleton frame structure . . . four stories in height, the uppermost being enclosed for a watchroom, . . . surmounted by a square lantern gallery and an octagonal fourth-order lantern. The keeper's dwelling, located some 100 feet south of the tower, is a one-and-a-half-story red brick building and extension. . . . The fog-signal building, located some 500 feet northeast of the tower, is a one-story frame structure covered with heavy sheathing and corrugated iron outside and smooth iron inside. The oil house is a brick house with a pitched roof.[77]

In the above photo (National Archives #26-LG-49-48) of the 1891 tower, a keeper appears to be drawing water from the lake with a winch. In 1898 the temporary tower was replaced by a permanent tower—a slender metal column surmounted by a lantern that held a third-order flashing lens, installed in 1901.

## Two Harbors Light Station (1892)

The Two Harbors Light Station was constructed on a point between Agate and Burlington Bays in Lake Superior in Minnesota. The lighthouse is a square two-story red brick building attached to a square brick tower. "Its fourth order lens guided iron ore carriers to Two Harbors, where they were loaded with iron ore [from the Mesabi Range]. The carriers then transported the ore to the furnaces of US Steel."[78] These images of the lighthouse and whistle and oil houses were taken by Herbert Bamber in 1893. (Courtesy of the USCG Historian's Office) The light station continues as an active aid to navigation in 1999.

Two Harbors Light Station

## St. George Reef Light Station (1892)

A lighthouse on this dangerous offshore reef eight miles northwest of
Crescent City, California, was first considered by the Light-House Board
in 1874. Funds were not appropriated until 1882, and were inadequate for
the difficult work required. Construction was started the following year on
the granite foundation, but the season during which men could work was
very short and funds kept running out. The structure proved the most
expensive ever undertaken by the Lighthouse Service ($726,000) and took
10 years to complete. All the stone had to quarried and cut on the
mainland and transported from Humboldt Bay by ship. Treacherous
storms halted the work; high waves swept away material and injured
workmen (one drowned). Work done the previous season often had to be
repaired before new work could go forward.

The 146-foot tower, the tallest on the West Coast, was designed by George
Ballantyne. The metal work of the lantern was made by the Phoenix Iron
Company in Trenton, New Jersey, and shipped to San Francisco. A first-
order lens was shipped from France and first lit in 1892.

St. George Reef Light Station

The above photo shows construction of the lighthouse as it neared completion. (National Archives #26-LG-66-37) The station was closed in 1975 when the light was replaced by a large navigational buoy.

## Three Sisters Light Station (1892)

Three short brick towers built in 1838 marked the sandbars off Nauset Beach in Massachusetts for the local fishing fleet and for coastal vessels. The only triple light station in the United States, they were easily distinguished from the single Cape Cod light to the north and the twin lights at Chatham to the south. Sixth-order lenses were installed in 1858, then changed to fourth-order in 1873. A wooden dwelling for the keeper was constructed in 1875.

THE U.S. LIGHT-HOUSE BOARD ACHIEVES ITS GOALS

Erosion ate away the bluff on which the towers stood. In 1892 they were replaced further inland by the wooden towers shown here, with the lanterns and lenses removed from the old towers. By 1911 erosion again threatened the Three Sisters. Two were extinguished and sold to a local resident for summer cottages. The third was moved next to the keeper's dwelling and attached by a covered walkway. It immediately had to be stabilized with guywires.

In 1923 one of the taller twin lights at Chatham was discontinued and moved to Nauset Beach, where it displayed a triple flash to honor the lost trio.[79] The third tower of the Three Sisters was also moved to be used as a cottage. When Cape Cod National Seashore was established in the 1960s, the Park Service purchased the little towers. In the 1980s they were stabilized, placed in their original configuration. They are now used as an interpretive exhibit. (National Archives #26-LG-8-68B)

## Heceta Head Light Station (1894)

Heceta Head Light Station was established near the mouth of the Suislaw River to light the dark Oregon coast between Cape Arago and Cape Foulweather. Using the same plans as the Umpqua station being constructed farther south along the coast, this station consisted, in addition to the tower, of two oil houses, a barn, a single dwelling for the principal keeper, and a duplex for the assistant keepers. Bringing materials to the site was extremely difficult—some of the lumber for construction was transported by tug, thrown overboard, and floated ashore. Although the tower was completed in August 1893, lighting the first-order lens was delayed until after the lamp arrived from the general depot in Staten Island, New York, in February 1894.[80] The station continues as an active aid to navigation in Suislaw National Forest. (National Archives #26-LG-71-85)

# Rawley Point Light Station (1894)

In response to a query from Stephen Pleasonton in 1850 as to whether a lighthouse was needed at Twin Rivers (the town nearest Rawley Point) on Lake Michigan in Wisconsin, the Superintendent of Lights in Buffalo wrote as follows:

> I would remark that for purposes of <u>general navigation</u> [*sic*], in my opinion it is not needed, for the <u>reason</u> [*sic*] that it is only six miles distant from Manitowoc Light, which could be discovered nearly as soon as the one at Twin Rivers . . . Twin Rivers, however, is an enterprising village of some 500 inhabitants, and a light might be of some benefit as a <u>local one</u> [*sic*] . . . It is my opinion, however, that if government commences to construct and keep up <u>local lights</u> [*sic*], there will be no end to the applications . . .[81]

Regardless of this response, the first aid was established shortly thereafter (1853) on Rawley Point and consisted of four poles that permitted a lantern to be hoisted about 75 feet in the air. Lake traffic must have increased substantially, for a new brick tower was constructed in 1873. In 1893 the top part of the brick tower was removed and the bottom floors incorporated into keepers' quarters for three families. The replacement skeleton-tower lighthouse erected near the dwelling was sent from the 1893 World's Fair. A central cylinder contained a spiral stairway to the lantern where a third-order Fresnel lens revolved on a steel roller by means of weights that were wound up every six hours.[82] The three keepers worked eight-hour shifts daily. The fog signal had to be tended throughout the day and night in bad weather.

Rawley Point Light continues as an active aid to navigation. (Courtesy of the USCG Historian's Office)

---

## Fourteen Mile Point Light Station (1894)

The 1892 *Annual Report* stated that "this prominent point is about 15 miles east of Ontonagon Light on Lake Superior, nearly at the limit of its visibility. There is no light in the southwest direction until that at Portage Lake Ship Canal is reached, a distance of more than 40 miles. A new coast light is needed here in the interests of a large commerce to and from Ashland Bay. All this commerce passes directly by Fourteen-Mile Point on the way to and from Keweenaw Point." This Michigan tower, brick duplex dwelling, fog-signal building, boathouse, and brick oil house were completed in 1894. The station originally had a Fresnel lens rotated by a clockwork mechanism that alternately flashed red and white. (National Archives #26-LG-50-40) Deactivated in the 1930s, the station was severely vandalized in the 1980s.

# Marblehead Light Station (1896)

A short wooden lighthouse was erected on Marblehead Neck in Massachusetts Bay in 1838. This tower is shown below with an old-style lantern. (Courtesy of the USCG Historian's Office) The low tower was obscured by surrounding development and was supplemented with a tall mast and hanging lantern. The 1893 *Annual Report* indicated that many types of vessels used this light to guide them into Marblehead's deep harbor,

> especially the fishermen, who, from the very nature of their business, find it necessary to enter and leave the harbor at any and all times, at night as well as by day. Many merchant vessels loaded with coal and general merchandise ply between this and other ports along the shore, and scores of yachts, with hundreds of pleasure seekers, make this their headquarters during the summer.

The images on the next page show the tower before and during the construction of a pyramidal skeletal tower. Note the temporary tower in the center of the bottom image. (National Archives #26-LG-8-1 and #26-LG-8-5B) The completed 100-foot tower shown on page 266 was lighted April 17, 1896, and remains active. (National Archives #26-LG-8-5A)

THE U.S. LIGHT-HOUSE BOARD ACHIEVES ITS GOALS

Marblehead Light Station

---

## Braddock Point Light Station (1896)

The Braddock Point Light on the New York shore of Lake Ontario near Hilton was lighted in 1896 with a third-and-one-half-order lens—the brightest on Lake Ontario. It lies between Thirty Mile Point Light and Oswego Light. The station is actually located on Bogus Point, three miles west of Braddock Point. The keeper's dwelling, tower, and woodshed were completed in 1895, the brick barn and metal oil house in 1896. The architect, Lt. Col. Jared A. Smith, copied the Cleveland Light (torn down in 1895), from which the ornate brass lantern, Fresnel lens, and metal work were transferred.[83] In 1899 a 270-degree lens replaced the 180-degree third-and-a-half-order lens. In 1902 leakage in the tower was stopped by removing and replacing the entire lantern, lantern deck, parapet gallery deck and rails, and all connecting iron work. A lens-lantern was exhibited from the north face of the tower while these repairs were going on.

The station was decommissioned in 1954. Because of structural damage, the Coast Guard removed the upper two-thirds of the tower. A private owner purchased the station in 1957.[84] (National Archives #26-LG-43-33)

Braddock Point Light Station

# North Head Light Station (1898)

North Head Light, shown here, was built in 1898 north of the mouth of the Columbia River in Washington on the ocean side of Cape Disappointment. Its 65-foot tower lofted the first-order lens transferred from the Cape Disappointment Light (which was in a poor location for guiding commerce and received a fourth-order replacement). The contractor who was to furnish the metal work was 173 days late in completing the construction, incurring a penalty that exceeded what he was to be paid. Because he was not responsible for the delay in receiving needed materials, he was given a three-month extension. Before the lighthouse was completed, the tower contractor sued the U.S. government to recover damages that he claimed to have sustained because of the delay in the delivery of the metal work beyond the time specified.

In 1939 the Coast Guard moved the first-order lens to the Fort Canby Interpretive Center, replacing it with a fourth-order lens. North Head was automated in 1961[85] and is now an active aid to navigation in Fort Canby State Park. (Courtesy of The Mariners' Museum, Newport News, Virginia)

*Grand River Beacon on Lake Erie in Fairport, Ohio. (National Archives #26-LG-45-44)*

# Conclusion

The lighthouse system continued to expand during the twentieth century. Puerto Rico's lighthouses came under the jurisdiction of the United States in 1900 and the first stations in Alaska were established in 1902. Concrete and steel, because they are very durable, became popular construction materials for lighthouses soon after the turn of the century. Many new designs displayed an Art Deco influence, but the towers were generally very utilitarian in style. The nineteenth century had seen the evolution of a number of different building styles, materials, and technology, but the twentieth century brought the demise of the lighthouse keeper position and the evolution of new navigational systems which made the old towers optional as aids to navigation.

The U.S. Light-House Board was abolished and the Bureau of Lighthouses created in 1910. Finally in 1939, lighthouses came under the jurisdiction of the U.S. Coast Guard. The Coast Guard did not construct many traditional lighthouses. With the increasing use of acetylene and electricity, the trend toward automation had begun. Navigational equipment was improving; the era in which ships relied on lighthouses for charting their courses was coming to a close.

Today all but one light station, Boston Harbor in Massachusetts, are automated and require only intermittent attention by the U.S. Coast Guard. New technology has eliminated the need for official keepers, but many non-Coast Guard caretakers have taken on the responsibility of maintaining and preserving these historic structures. The job is a challenging one. Located in harsh marine environments, often in isolated locations, these structures were built to withstand rough weather conditions and needed the daily care of a live-in keeper who saw to the cleaning, painting, caulking, ventilating, and other tasks vital to protecting the structure. When a steel pole or buoy works just as well as an aid to navigation, the Coast Guard cannot provide this kind of meticulous care.

The preservation of lighthouses is not a simple matter. In 1852, in a critique of the state of the U.S. system of lighthouses, the U.S. Light-House Board stated,

> With the exception of works designed to resist the fire of heavy batteries, there are, perhaps, among the higher class of structures, none that require so careful a selection of materials, nor greater professional knowledge, care, and skill in their preparation and combination, than is

required in the building of works exposed to the shock of the sea, or even in those, which, near the ocean, receive only the slow attacks of time and of the weather; and most especially is this true of *light-houses* built in such situations. Their small bases, great height, and naked exposure, subject them, in an eminent degree, to the influence of the causes which operate everywhere to the destruction of artificial works, and especially where they are exposed to the waves, to the spray, or even to the sea atmosphere.

Many of the light stations portrayed in this book no longer exist. Some of those that do are admired as engineering feats; others are seen as picturesque or romantic symbols of a more rugged era; others provide opportunities for important educational programs. Many lighthouses today are simply arresting landmarks in beautiful seascape settings, but they evoke memories of the very human determination to save lives and guide the mariner into safe havens. These historic light stations, cherished by the local community and nation alike, beg for protection so that they can serve in the decades to come as permanent reminders of our rich maritime heritage.

# Appendix

Excerpts from the 1846 *Report on Investigation of the Lighthouse Establishment*[1]

Navy Lieutenants Thornton A. Jenkins and Richard Bache were assigned a special detail "to procure information which may tend to the improvement of the light-house system of the United States;"[2] requiring travel to Great Britain and France to study the improvements made in those systems. Particular attention was paid to the organization of the lighthouse system, construction of lighthouses, and the lighting apparatus. The following are excerpts from the resulting report:

> It has been most clearly demonstrated to our minds, that an engineer of undoubted professional ability *is absolutely indispensable to a properly organized Light-House Establishment;* . . . ignorance in the selection of sites; large amounts required annually for repairs; badly constructed light-houses; shipwreck, with all its attendant horrors of loss of life and property, are a few of the evils consequent upon this neglect to employ a responsible person of acknowledged ability to fill a station of so much importance as that of engineer to the Light-house Department . . .
>
> It will be seen that very great care is taken to obtain the best oil, subjecting it to the best known tests, and a proper quantity allowed to

warrant keepers obeying strictly their instructions as to the time of lighting in the evening and extinguishing in the morning . . . The duties of the keeper should be most rigidly enforced. No keeper should be permitted to decide when is the proper time to light or extinguish his lights, but should be instructed to light his lamps at sunset, and keep the flames at their most effective height until sunrise. A failure to perform this duty strictly should be sufficient warrant for his removal.

> The examinations which we have made in relation to the advantages and disadvantages arising from the use of different modes of illumination, have convinced us of the very great superiority of the Fresnel apparatus to all others, and we cannot too strongly recommend its introduction to our light-houses.
>
> The higher orders of dioptric lights require *two keepers*, and we consider it equally important that this number should be allowed to all sea-coast and other first-class lights. In this opinion we are sustained by the practice of the whole of maritime Europe. . . .No sea-coast or other first-class light should ever be left between the times of lighting and extinguishing without a keeper. The draught of air in the lanterns increases and decreases with the force of the wind outside of the tower, thus rendering it

necessary to change the height of the wicks . . . in fact, the whole time of one person will be fully and profitably employed in keeping the flames, glass chimneys, and glass of the lanterns, and the other necessary fixtures of the light-room, in proper order.

A systematic arrangement of all the lights on the coast, giving to each a positively distinctive appearance, can alone fulfil all the wants of a difficult and hazardous navigation.

We . . . recommend the reorganization of our Light-house Establishment, by the appointment of an engineer, an optician, and a proper number of district superintendents, to assist the general superintendent of lights, buoys, and beacons, under the direction and control of the Secretary of the Treasury.

Under this organization the duties of the general superintendent would remain pretty much as they are at present; those of the engineer (who might be detailed with propriety from the Army) would be to make all plans, drawings, and specifications of works, assist in the selection of sites, superintend the construction and repairs of all towers, buildings, etc., inspect at least once a year the principal light-stations, report the condition of the lights, and suggest such improvements and repairs as he may deem proper and necessary. The duties of the optician would be to superintend the construction of and to test all illuminating apparatus and combustibles for light-house purposes, visit all the lights at least once a year, with the view to directing the adjustments and repairs of the fixtures of the lanterns, etc.

The coast should be divided into districts, and each district placed under an officer of the Navy—a superintendent of light-houses, light-vessels, buoys, and beacons. Eight or ten superintendents would be required to perform faithfully and successfully all the duties of this service—say eight on the Atlantic and Gulf coasts, and two on the lakes. Each of these superintendents should be supplied with a small vessel, to enable them to inspect, at least once every month, the floating lights, light-houses inaccessible by land, and all the buoys and beacons in their districts.

We would further recommend that a depot for oil, spare buoys, moorings, and other supplies, be established in each of the proposed districts, and placed under the charge of the district superintendents. There should not be less than two keepers to each of the sea-coast and first-class lights, and they should never be allowed to be left, after lighting in the evening at sun setting, until extinguished in the morning at sunrising, without a keeper. The keepers should be furnished with printed general and detailed instructions, similar to those supplied to keepers of the European lights. These general instructions should be printed in large type, on single sheets, framed, and hung up in the keepers' dwellings, and in the trimming rooms of the towers. They should embrace all the most important points of duty, such as the times for lighting and extinguishing the lights; the times for cleaning and preparing the lamps, reflectors, or other apparatus for lighting in the evening; general routine duty in the lantern at night; journals; returns of oil expending daily; quarterly returns, etc.

[We] recommend the appointment of a commission, to classify and arrange systematically, with reference to their order, range, and distinctive characteristics, all lights at present existing on our coasts, those proposed to be erected in localities already designated, and to examine into such other subjects relating to the light-houses, buoys, and beacons, and their management . . .

We would suggest that this temporary commission be composed of the general superintendent of lights, buoys, and beacons, as president, the superintendent of the survey of the coast, two officers of the Navy, of rank and experience, one military and one topographical engineer from the Army, and a junior officer of the Navy as secretary to the commission.

We believe this board would, upon examining into the subject, recommend a reduction of the number of lamps and reflectors at present employed in nearly all of harbor and other inland lights; if, indeed, the use of reflectors should not be abandoned for the more economical and equally efficient smaller classes of French lens lights, thereby greatly lessening the expense of maintenance, without in any manner diminishing the power and useful effects of the lights. Another, and a much more important point, would be gained by the appointment of this commission—that of obtaining an increased power, range, and efficiency in our sea-coast and other first-class lights, by an addition to the number, and an increased size of the reflectors; the employment of Argand lamps and burners, of the latest and most approved construction; and by the gradual and judicious introduction of the dioptric or Fresnel apparatus, with improved revolving machinery, lanterns, ventilators, etc. Another and a most important duty, which would devolve upon this board, would be to classify all the lights, and introduce such a number of distinctions into our system as to forbid the possibility of one light being mistaken for another; to examine and report upon all the petitions for new lights; decide upon the necessary power, range, and the proper distinctions to be given to those proposed to be established, etc.

The attention of this board should be particularly directed to the wants of our coasts, bays, rivers, and inlets, from Cape Henry to the Rio del Norte, a distance along the seaboard of nearly 2,500 miles, and upon which there are at present but fifty-six lights of all classes and descriptions, to guide the thousands of vessels freighted with the millions of dollars' worth of the products of our western, southwestern, and northwestern States, which pass annually through the Gulf and Florida pass, along one of most intricate and dangerous sea tracks known to navigators. The great northern and northwestern lakes, with their immense and daily increasing commerce, would also claim especial attention.

In concluding this part of our report, we beg leave to say that our conclusions have been arrived at after a patient and laborious investigation of the whole subject, so far as our time and means have permitted, and that the changes which we have proposed, or some other equally important ones, are absolutely necessary, to place our lights, buoys, and beacons in a proper state of efficiency, to compare favorably with those of the other maritime countries of the world, and thereby fulfil, as perfectly as may be, the laudable purposes for which they are designed.

*Outer Island Light Station, Apostle Islands, Lake Superior, Wisconsin. (National Archives # 26-LG-51-64)*

ENDNOTES

# ENDNOTES

## Introduction

[1]The 1,228 number is based on the number of "lighthouses and lighted beacons" listed in the 1900 *Annual Report*. The 650 number is based on a survey of light stations listed in the 1901 *Light Lists* or *List of Lights and Fog Signals on the Atlantic and Gulf Coasts of the United States, List of Lights and Fog Signals on the Pacific Coast of the United States...*, and *List of Lights and Fog Signals of the United States on the Northern Lakes and Rivers...* (Washington, D.C.: Government Printing Office, 1901)

## Part I. Lighthouses Under A New Nation

[1]These were Boston, MA; Brant Point, MA; Beavertail, RI; Sandy Hook, NJ (the only site where the original tower is still extant; the other surviving stations in this list are currently lit with later towers); Cape Henlopen, DE (station no longer extant); Charleston (Morris Island), SC; New London, CT; Plymouth, MA; Portsmouth, NH; Cape Ann, MA; Nantucket (Great Point), MA; and Newburyport Harbor, MA. Portland Head, ME, was under construction.

[2]F. Ross Holland, *America's Lighthouses* (New York: Dover Publications, 1972), p. 69.

[3]Ibid.

[4]D. Alan Stevenson, *The World's Lighthouses Before 1820* (London: Oxford University Press, 1959), p. 87.

[5]Arnold Burges Johnson, *Modern Light-House Service* (Washington, D.C.: Government Printing Office, 1890), p. 25.

[6]James Marston Fitch, *American Building 1: The Historical Forces That Shaped It* (Boston: Houghton Mifflin Company, 1966), p. 13.

[7]Johnson, p. 25.

[8]Discussed in Chapter 2.

[9]"Report of I.W.P. Lewis, Civil Engineer, made by order of Hon. W. Forward, Secretary of the Treasury, on the condition of light-houses, beacons, buoys, and navigation, upon the coasts of Maine, New Hampshire, and Massachusetts, in 1842," in U.S. Light-House Establishment, *Public Documents and Extracts from Reports and Papers Relating to Light-Houses, Light-Vessels, and Illumination Apparatus, and to Beacons, Buoys, and Fog Signals, 1789-1871* (Washington, D.C.: Government Printing Office, 1871), hereafter referred to as *Lighthouse Papers*, p. 356.

[10]Ibid., p. 357.

[11]Ralph W. Hammett, *Architecture in the United States: A Survey of Architectural Styles Since 1776* (New York: John Wiley & Sons, Inc., 1976), p. 41.

[12]Holland, *America's Lighthouses*, p.14.

[13] W. Branford Shubrick, President; Joseph G. Totten, Brevet Brigadier General; James Kearny, Lt. Col., Topographical Engineers; F. S. Dupont, Cdr., U.S. Navy; and A.D. Bache & Thornton A. Jenkins, Lts., U.S. Navy, "Report of the Light-House Board," January 30, 1852, in *Lighthouse Papers*.

[14]Some of the colonial lights were actually built and maintained with fees paid by the ship owners using that harbor.

[15] Letter dated April 24, 1849, from Stephen Pleasonton to the Secretary of the Treasury explaining how the construction of lighthouses is contracted and overseen (National Archives, Record Group 26, Entry 35, "Light-House Letters," Series P, 1833-1864). National Archives, Record Group 26 will hereafter be abbreviated NA, RG 26.

[16]Letter dated April 27, 1843, from Winslow Lewis (NA, RG 26, Entry 35, "Light-House Letters," Series P, 1833-1864).

[17]Report of Lieut. Geo. M. Bache, U.S.N., found in *Lighthouse Papers*, p. 209.

[18] Holland, *America's Lighthouses*, p. 152.

[19] NA, RG 26, Entry 17A, "Letters Received by the Treasury Department, 1785-1812."

[20] Lists of lighthouses were not kept on a systematic basis until after the formation of the U.S. Light-House Board in 1851; however, lists were generated beginning in the late 1830s. The titles varied somewhat, *List of Light-Houses, Lighted-Beacons, and Floating Lights of the United States* was used in the second half of the nineteenth century until the Great Lakes were put into a separate volume. We are using the generic reference, *Light List*.

[21] RG 26, Entry 17A, Volume 3, "Letters Received, Series F, 1804-1812, Pennsylvania & Southern States."

[22] Mary Louise Clifford and J. Candace Clifford, *Women Who Kept the Lights: An Illustrated History of Female Lighthouse Keepers* (Alexandria, Virginia: Cypress Communications, 1993), p. 168.

[23] Joseph Frankowski, "The Old Point Comfort Light," *Chesapeake Bay Magazine*, April 1985, p. 33; Benjamin H. Trask, "Two Points of Comfort," *The Keeper's Log*, Fall 1997, p. 8.

[24] Benjamin H. Trask, "New Point Comfort Light Station: The Other Point Comfort," *The Keeper's Log*, Fall 1997, p. 10.

[25] Robert Fraser, "Scituate Lighthouse," *The Keeper's Log*, Winter 1987, p. 3.

[26] Letter dated January 12, 1861, to the Secretary of the Treasury from James Buffington, House of Representatives (NA, RG 26, Entry 35, "Light-House Letters," Series P, 1851).

[27] NA, RG 26, Entry 6, "Annual Reports," 1851.

[28] Ibid.

[29] Ibid.

[30] NA, RG 26, Entry 19.

## Part II. Lighthouses Under the Fifth Auditor

[1] Lightships were placed in offshore locations where onshore towers could not adequately mark the hazard. Holland states that the first lightship, or light vessel, was stationed at Willoughby Spit, Virginia, in 1820; the first in the open seas was stationed at Sandy Hook, New Jersey, in 1823. Holland, *America's Lighthouses*, p.55.

[2] Johnson, p. 14, although Holland in *Great American Lighthouses* claims there were 331 lighthouses and 42 lightships in 1852.

[3] Holland, *America's Lighthouses*, p. 27.

[4] Hammett, p. 69.

[5] James Marston Fitch, p. 9.

[6] Shubrick, et al., "1852 Report of the Light-House Board," in *Lighthouse Papers*, p. 693.

[7] Robert Mills (Washington, D.C.: Thompson & Homans, 1832), pp. 178-182.

[8] Letter from James Rodgers to Stephen Pleasonton dated August 3, 1842; Rodgers wrote another letter dated February 18, 1843, suggesting cast iron for construction of Flynn's Knoll Lighthouse. This suggestion was also rejected (NA, RG 26, Entry 17F "Miscellaneous Letters Received").

[9] Shubrick, et al., "1852 Report of the Light-House Board," in *Lighthouse Papers*, p. 692.

[10] Professor Trowbridge, U.S. Coast Survey, Department of Commerce, "The Harbors, Bays, Islands, and Retreats, of the Gulf of Mexico," *DeBow's Review*, 1859, Volume 27, Issue 5, p. 596.

[11] David Cipra, *Lighthouses, Lightships, and the Gulf of Mexico* (Alexandria, Virginia: Cypress Communications, 1997), p. 7.

[12] Love Dean, *Lighthouses of the Florida Keys* (Sarasota, Florida: Pineapple Press, 1998), p. 22.

[13] Ibid., pp. 24-25.

[14] Hyde, pp. 15-16, 20.

[15] NA, RG 26, Entry 35, "Light-House Letters," Series P, 1843.

[16] Holland, *America's Lighthouses*, pp. 28-29.

[17] NA, RG 26, Entry 17F, "Miscellaneous Letters Received."

[18] Holland, *America's Lighthouses*, p. 18.

[19] NA, RG 26, Entry 17G, "Miscellaneous Letters Received," Box 7.

[20] Ibid.

[21] NA, RG 26, Entry 6, "Annual Reports," 1848.

[22] NA, RG 26, Entry 6, "Circular to Superintendents of Light Houses, 1838," with 1849 revisions.

[23] NA, RG 26, Entry 35, "Light-House Letters," Series P, 1848.

[24] Ibid.

[25] NA, RG 26, Entry 35, "Light-House Letters," Series P, 1850.

[26] NA, RG 26, Entry 35, "Light-House Letters," Series P, 1833-1864.

[27] Letter dated January 25, 1864 (NA, RG 26, Entry 35, "Light-House Letters," Series P, 1864).

[28] Hereafter abbreviated as *Annual Report*.

[29] Taken from "Schedule of the Light Houses and Beacons in the United States with the number of Lamps lit in each on the first day of January 1823" (NA, RG 26, Entry 6).

[30] Clifford and Clifford, pp. 11-15.

[31] Letter from E. Whitman, dated March 3, 1811 (NA, RG 26, Entry 17F).

[32] NA, RG 26, Entry 35, "Light-House Letters," Series P, 1833.

[33] Ibid.

[34] Ibid.

[35]NA, RG 26, Entry 17K, "Letters received from the Secretary of the Treasury," 1838.

[36]Spelled "Permelia" in some sources.

[37]Ross Holland, *Maryland Lighthouses of the Chesapeake Bay* (Crownsville, Maryland: Maryland Historical Society Press, 1997), p. 27.

[38]Capt. Derby of Revenue Cutter *Morris*, "Remarks on Light Houses," Aug. 16, 1831 (NA, RG 26, Entry 6).

[39]NA, RG 26, Entry 35, "Light-House Letters," Series P, 1843.

[40]Report from captain of the U. S. Revenue Cutter *Woodbury*, July 12, 1843, and request from New Orleans collector, November 9, 1836 (NA, RG 26, Entry 35).

[41]Mike Vogel, "Beacon to the Heartland," *The Keeper's Log*, Fall 1987, pp. 2-8.

[42]NA, RG 26, Entry 17F, "Miscellaneous Letters."

[43]Report of Lieutenant Edward W. Carpenter, U.S.N., New York, November 1, 1838, in *Lighthouse Papers*, p. 195.

[44]From log entry dated May 19, 1879, quoted in *The Keeper's Log*, Summer 1991, p. 320.

[45]Letter from Stephen Pleasonton to the Secretary of the Treasury dated October 1, 1838 (NA, RG 26, Entry 35).

[46]NA, RG 26, Entry 6, "Annual Reports," 1851.

[47]Letter dated May 22, 1837 (NA, RG 26, Entry 35).

[48]*Lighthouse Papers*, p. 357.

[49]Report dated July 1843, from Michael Connor, U.S. Revenue Cutter *Jackson* (NA, RG 26, Entry 35).

[50]Letter dated April 11, 1849, from Joshua Nickerson (NA, RG 26, Entry 35).

[51]Report dated July 1843, from Michael Connor, U.S. Revenue Cutter *Jackson* (NA, RG 26, Entry 35).

[52]Arthur E. Railton, "Cape Poge Light, Part II," *The Keeper's Log*, Summer 1994, pp. 11-18.

[53]NA, RG 26, Entry 17J, "Records Relating to the Library of Congress Exhibit, 1785-1852."

[54]NA, RG 26, Entry 17G, Box 3.

[55]NA, RG 26, Entry 17F, "Miscellaneous Letters Received."

[56]Ibid.

[57]An 1843 memo reported the following stations as having assistant keepers appointed by the government: Franks Island, LA; Bayou St. John, LA; South West Pass, LA; South Point, LA; Pleasonton's Island, LA; Cat Island, LA; Pass Manchac, LA; New Canal, LA; Vermillion Bay, LA; Dry Tortuga, FL; Sand Key, FL; Turtle Island, OH; and Navesink, NJ. Their salaries ranged from $100 to $360 per annum (NA, RG 26, Entry 17G, Box 7).

[58]Report of I.W.P. Lewis in *Lighthouse Papers*, p. 370.

[59]NA, RG 26, Entry 17K, "Letters Received from the Secretary of the Treasury," 1835.

[60]Several years later, Pleasonton struck out No. 6 of the Instructions and modified No. 7 to replace contractors with Superintendent.

## Part III. The U.S. Light-House Board Improves the System

[1]Holland, *America's Lighthouses*, pp. 34-36.

[2]Shubrick, et al., "1852 Report of the Light-House Board," in *Lighthouse Papers*, p. 628.

[3]Ibid., p. 631.

[4]Ibid., p. 639.

[5]Ibid., pp. 632-633, 635, 645, 647.

[6]Ibid, pp. 712-713.

[7]Robert Scheina, *Lighthouses: Then and Now*, supplement to *Commandant's Bulletin* (Washington, D.C.: U.S. Coast Guard, 1989), p. 6.

[8]Scheina, p. 6.

[9]Shubrick, et al., "1852 Report of the Light-House Board," in *Lighthouse Papers*, p. 632.

[10]The 193-foot height is from ground level to the top of the lantern; the entire structure from the base of its foundation is 206 feet tall according to 1989 documentation by the Historic American Buildings Survey.

[11]Scheina, p. 9.

[12]Holland, *America's Lighthouses*, pp. 20-21.

[13]The first transcontinental railroad was completed in 1869; a north-south route was not available until 1887.

[14]NA, RG 26, Entry 35, "Light-House Letters," Series P, 1833-1864.

[15]Wayne Wheeler, "The History of Fog Signals, Part II," *The Keeper's Log*, Fall 1990, pp. 8-10.

[16]Letter from Joseph Farwell, Light-House Inspector;1853 *Annual Report*.

[17]Johnson, p. 64.

[18]NA, RG 26, Entry 19, "Letters Sent by the Secretary of the Treasury," 1861.

[19]Ibid.

[20]Cipra, p. 20.

[21]George Weiss, *The Lighthouse Service: Its History, Activities and Organization* (Baltimore, Maryland: John Hopkins Press, 1926), p. 16.

[22]NA, RG 26, Entry 35, "Light-House Letters," Series P, 1843.

[23]Holland, *Great American Lighthouses*, p. 85.

[24]NA, RG 26, Entry 35, "Light-House Letters," Series P, 1851.

[25]NA, RG 26, Entry 17K, "Letters Received from the Secretary of the Treasury," 1851.

[26]NA, RG 26, Entry 17A, "Letters Received by the Treasury Department," 1805-1812.

[27]Wayne Wheeler, "The History of Fog Signals, Part 1," *The Keeper's Log,* Summer 1990, p. 22.

[28]NA, RG 26, Entry 17F, "Miscellaneous Letters Received."

[29]Ibid.

[30]1869 *Light List.*

[31]NA, RG 26, Entry 36, "Letters Received by the Light-House Service, 1829-1900," Box 107.

[32]NA, RG 26, Entry 35, "Light-House Letters," Series P, 1851.

[33]McCarthy, pp. 101-104.

[34]Cipra, p. 101.

[35]Ibid., p. 102.

[36]Clifford and Clifford, pp. 103-104.

[37]1887 *Annual Report.*

[38]Admont G. Clark, "Monomoy Point Lighthouse," *The Keeper's Log,* Spring 1991, pp. 12-15.

[39]Holland, *Maryland Lighthouses,* p. 53.

[40]NA, RG 26, Entry 35, "Light-House Letters," Series P, 1835.

[41]Cipra, p. 119.

[42]Clifford and Clifford, p. 160.

[43]NA, RG 26, Entry 35, "Light-House Letters," Series P, 1833-1864, Box 7.

[44]Major Hartman Bache's report, reproduced in the 1855 *Annual Report.*

[45]Clifford and Clifford, p. 44.

[46]Wayne Wheeler, personal communication, August 4,1999.

[47]Ibid., p. 25.

[48]Peter White, "The Farallones," *The Keeper's Log,* Fall 1988, p. 6.

[49]Ibid., p. 6.

[50]Ibid.

[51]Charles S. Green, "Los Farallones de los Frayles," *Overland Monthly and Out West Magazine,* Volume 20, Issue 117, 1892, p. 240; John A. Hussey, editor, "Farallon Islands Lighthouse," *Early West Coast Lighthouses* (San Francisco: Book Club of California, 1964), unpaged.

[52]Ibid, p. 244.

[53]Ibid.

[54]Hussey, unpaged.

[55]Peter White, "The Farallones," *The Keeper's Log,* Fall 1988, p. 11.

[56]Hussey, unpaged.

[57]1853 *Annual Report.*

[58]Ibid.

[59]1869 *Annual Report.*

[60]Personal correspondence from Patricia Grant dated May 13, 1996.

[61]Clifford and Clifford, pp. 22-29.

[62]1856 *Annual Report.*

[63]NA, RG 26, Entry 35, "Lighthouse Letters," Series P, 1833-1864.

[64]1883 *Annual Report.*

[65]James G. McCurdy, "Cape Flattery and Its Light," *Overland Monthly and Out West Magazine,* Volume 31, Issue 184, 1898, p. 349-50.

[66]Holland, *Great American Lighthouses,* p. 84.

[67]Ibid.

[68]NA, RG 26, Entry 35, "Light-House Letters," Box 1, April 1833-November 1837.

[69]Holland, *Great American Lighthouses,* p. 84.

[70]*Lighthouse Papers,* p. 204.

[71]Letter dated December 14, 1839, from Hon. Albert Smith (NA, RG 26, Entry 17F).

[72]R.G. Pendergrast, Lt., U.S.N., "Recapitulatory Report," August 18, 1837, in *Lighthouse Papers,* p. 82.

[73]1885 *Annual Report.*

[74]Dean, pp. 181-189.

[75]*Light List,* 1869.

[76]Elinor De Wire, "West Quoddy Head Light," in *Sentries Along the Shore* (Gales Ferry, Connecticut: Sentinel Publications, 1997), pp. 100-102.

[77]1873 *Annual Report.*

[78]1890 *Annual Report.*

[79]Holland, *Great American Lighthouses,* p. 315.

[80]*Light List,* 1898.

[81]"The Lighthouses of Lake Champlain," *The Keeper's Log,* Winter 1994, excerpted from the *Lake Champlain Album, Volume II* by Morris Glenn.

[82]Clifford and Clifford, pp. 61-73.

[83]Kevin M. McCarthy, *Florida Lighthouses* (Gainesville: University of Florida Press, 1990), p. 126.

[84]Cipra, p. 61.

[85]Keeper's report "Pensacola Light House at Barancas—Articles on hand 1st January 1828" (NA, RG 26, Entry 6).

[86]"State of the Light House at Pensacola, Fla, during the Year 1839" (NA, RG 26, Entry 6).

[87]1853 *Annual Report.*

[88]Cipra, p. 62.

[89]Ibid.

[90]1855 *Annual Report.*

[91]Cipra, pp. 97-98.

[92]Ibid.

[93]Holland, *Great American Lighthouses,* p. 208.

[94]*Light List,* 1849.

[95]Letter dated December 29, 1846, from Capt. Josiah Sturgis, USRS, to Stephen Pleasonton (NA, RG 26, Entry 17F).

[96]NA, RG 26, Entry 35, "Light-House Letters," Series P, 1833-1864.

[97]Letter from Joseph Sturgis, Capt, to Stephen Pleasonton, dated October 30, 1841 (NA, RG, 26, Entry 17F).

[98]NA, RG 26, Entry 17F, "Miscellaneous Letters Received."

[99]The lighthouse on the mainland continued in operation in spite of Pendergrast's recommendation (*Lighthouse Papers*, p. 83).

[100]The *Annual Report* of 1868 contradicts that of 1854 in stating that a fifth-order lens installed that year replaced a sixth-order lens.

[101]1873 *Annual Report*.

[102]NA, RG 26, Entry 17F, "Miscellaneous Letters Received."

[103]*Lighthouse Papers*, p. 754.

[104]1857 *Annual Report*.

[105]1868 *Annual Report*.

[106]1851 *Annual Report*.

[107]NA, RG 26, Entry 35, "Light-House Letters," Series P, 1863.

[108]NA, RG 26, Entry 35, "Light-House Letters," Series P, 1864.

[109]Shanks has an excellent chapter on Fort Point Light, pp. 105-127, on which this summary is based.

[110]NA, RG 26, Entry 35, "Light-House Letters," Series P, 1833-1864.

[111]NA, RG 26, Entry 17K, "Letters Received by the Secretary of the Treasury," 1843.

[112]Ibid.

[113]Ibid.

[114]Shubrick, et al., "1852 Report of the Light-House Board," in *Lighthouse Papers*, p. 643.

[115]George Worthylake, "The Depot," *The Keeper's Log*, Spring 1998, pp. 23-24.

[116]1867 *Annual Report*, pp. 17-18.

## Part IV. The U.S. Light-House Board Acheives Its Goals

[1]Johnson, p. 32.

[2]Johnson, pp.102-103.

[3]Johnson, pp.103-105.

[4]George R. Putnam, *Lighthouses and Lightships of the United States* (Boston: Houghton Mifflin Co., 1933), p. 238.

[5]Johnson, pp. 23, 54, 61.

[6]Numbers are based on those reported in the 1867, 1877, 1887, and 1897 *Annual Reports*.

[7]Johnson, p. 23.

[8]The boundary was reconfigured so that in 1897, the district extended from Hampton Harbor, NH, to Warren Point, RI.

[9]The boundary was reconfigured so that in 1897, the district extended from Warren Point, RI, to Shrewsbury Rocks, NJ, and included Lake Champlain.

[10]This number includes 96 post lights.

[11]Includes seven post lights.

[12]Includes six post lights.

[13]The boundary was reconfigured so that in 1897, the district extended from New River Inlet, NC, to Jupiter Inlet, FL.

[14]Includes 112 post lights.

[15]The boundary was reconfigured so that in 1897, the district extended from Jupiter Inlet, FL, to Perdido, FL.

[16]Includes 18 post lights.

[17]This number includes 30 stake-lights on the Columbia and Willamette Rivers.

[18]This number includes 94 post lights.

[19]In 1887, this number includes buoys in Alaskan waters.

[20]Johnson, p. 106.

[21]U.S. Treasury Department, *Organization and Duties of the Light-house Board; and Regulations, Instructions, Circulars, and General Orders of the Light-house Establishment of the United States* (Washington, D.C.: Government Printing Office, 1871), hereafter referred to as the *1871 Regulations*, pp. 54-55.

[22]*1871 Regulations*, p. 57.

[23]*1871 Regulations*, p. 61.

[24]Gredell & Associates: Structural Engineers, "Chesapeake Bay Lighthouses" (Wilmington, Delaware, 1991), p. 12.

[25]Ralph Eshelman, "Lighthouse Construction Types," unpublished ms drafted for the National Maritime Initiative through a cooperative agreement with the U.S. Lighthouse Society.

[26]Gredell & Associates, p. 12.

[27]1894 *Annual Report*.

[28]Johnson, pp. 37-40.

[29]Scheina, p. 23; Johnson, pp. 36-40.

[30]Report dated July 1843, from Michael Connor, U.S. Revenue Cutter *Jackson* (NA, RG 26, Entry 35).

[31]Letter dated December 27, 1873, from Superintendent of Lights, Detroit, to Secretary Richardson, (NA, RG 26, Entry 36, "Letters Received by the Lighthouse Service, 1829-1900," Box 8).

[32]"Letters Received from the District Engineers and Inspectors, 1853-1900" (NA, RG 26, Entry 24, Box 302).

[33]McCarthy, p. 29.

[34]NA, RG 26, Entry 35, "Light-House Letters," Series P, Box 5, 1833-1864.

[35]Frank M. Childers, *History of the Cape Canaveral Lighthouse* (The Brevard Museum, Inc., 1993), pp. 7-8, and 28. Some reports claim Burnham buried the

equipment, but it is more likely he hid it, as moisture would have caused major decay.

[36]1868 *Annual Report.*

[37]1869 *Annual Report.*

[38]Holland, *Great American Lighthouses*, p. 286.

[39] Dewey Livingston and David Snow, *The History and Architecture of the Point Reyes Light Station*, Historic Structures Report (Point Reyes: National Park Service, 1990), pp.5-36. The history section of this report draws heavily on Anna Toxe Toogood, *Historic Study: A Civil History of Golden Gate National Recreation Area and Point Reyes National Seashore, California* (Denver: Historic Preservation Branch, Pacific Northwest/Western Team, Denver Service Center, National Park Service, Department of the Interior, 1980; the *San Francisco Chronicle*; Shanks and Shanks, *Lighthouses and Lifeboats of the Redwood Coast* (San Anselmo: Costano Books, 1978); Light-House Board *Annual Reports*; etc.

[40]*Lighthouse Papers*, p. 785.

[41]James Tinney and Mary Burdette-Watkins, *Seaway Trail Lighthouses: An Illustrated Guide* (Sacketts Harbor, New York: Seaway Trail Foundation, Inc.,1997), p. 45.

[42]1869 *Annual Report.*

[43]1888 *Annual Report.*

[44]1889 *Annual Report.*

[45]1877 *Annual Report.*

[46]Holland, *Great American Lighthouses*, p. 183.

[47]Holland, *America's Lighthouses*, p. 118.

[48]1869 *Annual Report.*

[49]NA, RG 26, Entry 19, "Letters sent by the Secretary of the Treasury," April 1851-June 1878.

[50]1872 *Annual Report.*

[51]Ibid.

[52]Holland, *Maryland Lighthouses*, pp. 71-72.

[53]O.M. Poe, Major of Engineers, Member of U.S. Light-House Board, "Memoranda Concerning Spectacle Reef Light-House" (NA, RG 287, "Publications of the U.S. Government," Box T663).

[54]Ibid.

[55]Johnson, pp. 32-33.

[56]Holland, *Maryland Lighthouses*, p. 103.

[57]NA, RG 26, Entry 36, "Letters Received by the Light-House Service, 1829-1900," Box 122.

[58]NA, RG 26, Entry 6, "Annual Reports," Box 1.

[59]Holland, *Great American Lighthouses*, p. 188.

[60]1874 *Annual Report.*

[61]Dean, pp. 221-227.

[62]Ibid.

[63]NA, RG 26, Entry 17J, "Records Relating to the Library of Congress Exhibit, 1785-1852."

[64]1881 and 1882 *Annual Reports.*

[65]1872 *Annual Report.*

[66]1903 *Annual Report.*

[67]1880 *Annual Report.*

[68]1881 *Annual Report.*

[69]Holland, *Great American Lighthouses*, p. 249.

[70]McElbridge of U.S. Coast Guard Historical Section, "History of the Fort Point Light Station," 5/51.

[71]Ibid.

[72]Report of Charles W. Raymond, Major of Engineers, October 23, 1883, in *Lighthouse Papers*.

[73]Ralph Eshelman, "Ponce de Leon Inlet Light Station," National Historic Landmark study (National Park Service, National Historic Landmarks Survey, 1998), p. 5.

[74]Cipra, p. 103.

[75]George Worthylake, "Ballast Point, San Diego, California," *The Keeper's Log*, Summer 1997, pp. 34-35.

[76]1891 *Annual Report.*

[77]1892 *Annual Report.*

[78]Holland, *Great American Lighthouses*, p. 242.

[79]For further details, see Elinor de Wire, "Cape Cod's Three Sisters," *Mariners Weather Log*, Winter 1995.

[80]Stephanie Finucane, "Heceta House: A Historical and Architectural Survey," excerpted into an article, "Heceta Head: A Light Station Odyssey," *The Keeper's Log*, Spring 1992, pp. 2-4.

[81]NA, RG 26, Entry 17K, "Letters Received from the Secretary of the Treasury, 1830-1852."

[82]Timothy Harrison, "A Brief History of Rawley Point (Twin River Point) Lighthouse," in *International Lighthouse Magazine*, February 1996.

[83]Tinney and Burdette-Watkins, p. 23.

[84]Ibid.

[85]Holland, *Great American Lighthouses*, pp. 307-308.

## *Appendix*

[1]Thornton A. Jenkins, Lt., U.S. Navy, and Rich. Bache, Lt., U.S. Navy, "Report to Hon. R.J. Walker, Secretary of the Treasury," (Washington City, June 22, 1846) in *Lighthouse Papers*, pp. 448-465.

[2]*Lighthouse Papers*, p. 446.

# BIBLIOGRAHY

## Published Sources

Bradbury, Thomas, "The Guardian of the Harbor"in *Kennebunkport Conservation Trust Newsletter*, Fall/Winter 1993

Carse, Robert, *Keepers of the Lights: A History of American Lighthouses* (New York: Charles Scribners & Sons, 1968)

Childers, Frank M., *History of the Cape Canaveral Lighthouse* (The Brevard Museum, Inc., 1993)

Cipra, David L., *Lighthouses, Lightships, and the Gulf of Mexico* (Alexandria, Virginia: Cypress Communications, 1997)

Clark, Admont G., "Monomoy Point Lighthouse," in *The Keeper's Log*, Spring 1991

Clemensen, A. Berle, William W. Howell, Historic Structures Report, *Three Sisters Lighthouse, Cape Cod National Seashore, Massachsetts* (US Dept of Interior/NPS, 1984)

Clifford, Candace, editor, *1994 Inventory of Historic Light Stations* (Washington, D.C.: National Park Service, National Maritime Initiative, 1994); see web site for latest version of the computerized inventory at <http://www.cr.nps.gov/maritime/ltsum.htm>

Clifford, Mary Louise and J. Candace, *Women Who Kept the Lights: An Illustrated History of Female Lighthouse Keepers* (Alexandria, Virginia: Cypress Communications, 1993)

de Wire, Elinor, "Cape Cod's Three Sisters," in *Mariners Weather Log*, Winter 1995

_____, *Guardians of the Lights* (Sarasota, Florida: Pineapple Press, Inc., 1995)

_____, *The Lighthouse Keeper's Scrapbook* (Sentinel Press, 1994)

Dean, Love, *Lighthouses of the Florida Keys* (Sarasota, Florida: Pineapple Press, 1998)

Finucane, Stephanie, "Heceta House: A Historical and Architectural Survey" excerpted into an article, "Heceta Head: A Light Station Odyssey," in *The Keeper's Log*, Spring 1992

Fitch, James Marston, *American Building 1: The Historical Forces That Shaped It* (Boston: Houghton Mifflin Company, 1966)

Frankowski, Joseph, "The Old Point Comfort Light," in *Chesapeake Bay Magazine,* April 1985

Fraser, Robert, "Scituate Lighthouse," in *The Keeper's Log*, Winter 1987

Green, Charles S., "Los Farallones de los Frayles," in *Overland Monthly and Out West Magazine*, Volume 20, Issue 117, 1892

Hammett, Ralph W., *Architecture in the United States: A Survey of Architectural Styles Since 1776* (New York: John Wiley & Sons, Inc., 1976)

Harrison, Timothy, "A Brief History of Rawley Point (Twin River Point) Lighthouse," in *International Lighthouse Magazine*, February 1996

Holden, Melville, "Guardians at the Golden Gate," in *Westways*, March 1961

Holland, Francis Ross, Jr., *America's Lighthouses: An Illustrated History* (New York: Dover Publications, Inc., 1972)

_____, *Great American Lighthouses* (Washington, D.C.: The Preservation Press, 1989)

_____, *Maryland Lighthouses of the Chesapeake Bay* (Crownsville, Maryland: Maryland Historical Society Press, 1997)

Hornberger, Patrick, and Linda Turbyville, *Forgotten Beacons: The Lost Lighthouses of the Chesapeake Bay* (Annapolis, Maryland: Eastwind Publishing, 1997)

Hussey, John A., editor, "Farallon Islands Lighthouse," in *Early West Coast Lighthouses* (San Francisco: Book Club of California, 1964)

Hyde, Charles K., *The Northern Lights: Lighthouses of the Upper Great Lakes* (Lansing, Michigan: Two Peninsula Press)

Johnson, Arnold Burges, Chief Clerk, U.S. Light-House Board, *The Modern Light-House Service* (Washington, D.C.: Government Printing Office, 1890)

*Light Lists* titled *Light-Houses , &c. of the United States; List of Light-Houses, Beacons, and Floating Lights of the United States; List of Light-Houses, Lighted Beacons, and Floating Lights of the Atlantic, Gulf, and Pacific Coasts of the United States;* and *List of Light-Houses, Lighted Beacons, and Floating Lights of the Atlantic, Gulf, and Pacific Coasts of the United States* (facsimiles produced by the Nautical Research Centre, Petaluma, California)

McCarthy, Kevin M., *Florida Lighthouses* (Gainesville: University of Florida Press, 1990)

McCurdy, James G., "Cape Flattery and Its Light," in *Overland Monthly and Out West Magazine*, Volume 31, Issue 184, 1898

Mills, Robert, *The American Pharos or Lighthouse Guide*, founded on official reports received at the Treasury Department; also, a general view of the coast from the St. Lawrence to the Sabine, to which is added an appendix containing an account of the lighthouses on the Gulf and River St. Lawrence, with sailing directions for the St. Lawrence (Washington, D.C.: Thompson & Homans, 1832). This document lists all the lighthouses extant in 1832 and gives directions for mariners approaching them.

Noble, Dennis L., *Lighthouses & Keepers: The U.S. Lighthouse Service and Its Legacy* (Annapolis, Maryland: Naval Institute Press, 1997)

Putnam, George R., *Lighthouses and Lightships of the United States* (Boston: Houghton Mifflin Co., 1933)

Railton, Arthur R., "Cape Poge Light, Remote and Lonely," in *The Keeper's Log*, Spring, Summer, Fall, Winter 1994

Robert Scheina, *Lighthouses: Then and Now*, supplement to *Commandant's Bulletin*, 1989

Shanks, Ralph, *Guardians of the Golden Gate* (Petaluma, California: Costano Books, 1990)

Stevenson, D. Alan, *World's Lighthouses Before 1820* (London: Oxford University Press, 1959)

Taylor, Thomas W., *The Beacon of Mosquito Inlet: A History of the Ponce de Leon Inlet Lighthouse* (self-published 1993)

Tinney, James, and Mary Burdette-Watkins, *Seaway Trail Lighthouses: An Illustrated Guide* (Sacketts Harbor, New York: Seaway Trail Foundation, Inc., 1997)

Trowbridge, Professor, U.S. Coast Survey, Department of Commerce, "The Harbors, Bays, Islands, and Retreats, of the Gulf of Mexico," in *DeBow's Review*, 1859, Volume 27, Issue 5

Trask, Benjamin H., "Two Points of Comfort" and "New Point Comfort Light Station," in *The Keeper's Log*, Fall 1997

U.S. Coast Guard, *Historically Famous Lighthouses* (Washington, D.C.)

U.S. Light-House Establishment, *Public Documents and Extracts from Reports and Papers Relating to Light-Houses, Light-Vessels, and Illumination Apparatus, and to Beacons, Buoys, and Fog Signals, 1789-1871* (Washington, D.C.: Government Printing Office, 1871)

U.S. Treasury Department, *Annual Reports of the Light-House Board*, (Washington, D.C.)

U.S. Treasury Department, *Organization and Duties of the Light-house Board; and Regulations, Instructions, Circulars, and General Orders of the Light-house Establishment of the United States* (Washington, D.C.: Government Printing Office, 1871)

Vogel, Mike, "Beacon to the Heartland," in *The Keeper's Log*, Fall 1987

Weiss, George, *The Lighthouse Service: Its History, Activities and Organization* (Baltimore, MD: John Hopkins Press, 1926)

Wheeler, Wayne, "The History of Fog Signals, Part I" in *The Keeper's Log,* Summer 1990

_____, "The History of Fog Signals, Part II," in *The Keeper's Log,* Fall 1990

White, Peter, "The Farallones," in *The Keeper's Log*, Fall 1988

Worthylake, George, "Ballast Point, San Diego, California," in *The Keeper's Log*, Summer 1997

_____ , "The Depot," *The Keeper's Log,* Spring 1998

### Unpublished Sources

Eshelman, Ralph, "Historical Overview and Significance Evaluation, Point Lookout Light Station" as part of a condition assessment report completed by the National Park Service for the Department of Defense Legacy Management Program, 1995-1996

_____, "Lighthouse Construction Types," unpublished manuscript prepared for the National Maritime Initiative, National Park Service, through a cooperative agreement with the U.S. Lighthouse Society, 1996

_____, "Ponce de Leon Inlet Light Station," National Historic Landmark study (National Park Service, National Historic Landmarks Survey, 1998)

Gredell & Associates: Structural Engineers, "Chesapeake Bay Lighthouses" (Wilmington, Delaware, 1991)

Livingston, Dewey, and David Snow, "The History and Architecture of the Point Reyes Light Station," Historic Structures Report (Point Reyes: National Park Service, 1990)

National Archives, Record Group 26 (NA, RG 26), "Records of the U.S. Coast Guard, 1785-1988" (Washington, D.C.)

National Archives, Record Group 287, "Publications of the U.S. Government, 1790-1979" (Washington, D.C.)

National Register Nomination, "Little River Light Station," Light Stations of Maine MPS, Washington County, Maine (on file in the National Register of Historic Places, National Park Service, 1988)

National Register Nomination, "Long Island Head Light," Lighthouses of Massachusetts Thematic Group Nomination, Suffolk County, Massachusetts (On file in the National Register of Historic Places, National Park Service, 1981)

National Register Nomination, "Hendricks Head Light Station," Light Stations of Maine MPS, Lincoln County, Maine (on file in the National Register of Historic Places, National Park Service, 1987)

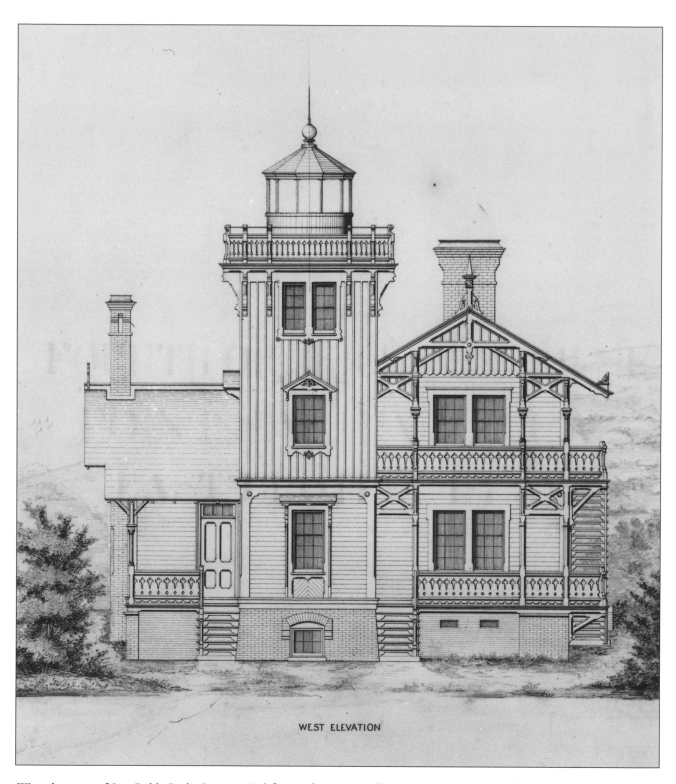

WEST ELEVATION

*West elevation of San Pablo Light Station, California, by George Elliot, 1872. (National Archives)*

# INDEX

## A

Abert, I.I. 92
Admiralty Head Light Station 162
Agate Bay, Minnesota 256
Alcatraz Island, California 80
Alcatraz Light Station 103, 170
American Revolution 6, 65, 123
American Shoal Light Station 236-237
American Society of Civil Engineering Landmark 159
Annapolis Harbor, Maryland 73
Apostle Islands, Wisconsin 255, 276
Appalachee Bay, Florida 64
Argand, Ami 4
Army of the Potomac 196
Ashland Bay, Michigan 262
Ashtabula Harbor Light Station 52-53

## B

Bache, George M. 88, 132
Bache, Hartman 92, 118
Back River Light Station 36-37
Bailey Island, Maine 209
Bakers Island Light Station 29
Bald Head Light Station 29
Ballantyne, George 257
Ballast Point Light Station 254
Baltimore, Maryland 110
Bamber, Herbert 2, 15, 31, 38, 64, 97, 130, 143, 152, 162, 205, 206, 209, 215, 226, 241, 245, 254, 256
Barnegat Light Station 246
Bates, Rebecca and Abigail 14
Bates, Simeon 14
Battery Point Light Station 80
Bay Islands State Park 132
Bay of Fundy, Maine 140
Beavertail Light Station 81, 190

Beck, Charles 67
Belle Isle Light Station 243
Bergen Point Light Station 151
Bethel, Joseph 137
Billingsgate Island Light Station 29, 61
Biloxi Light Station 70
Bird Island Light Station 19-20, 29
Bishop and Clerks Light Station 144-145
Black River Light Station 125-127
Black Rock Harbor Light Station 30
Black Rock Range Light Station 100-101
Block Island Southeast Light Station 228
Bloody Point Bar Light Station 189
Bluff Point Light Station 223
boats at stations 4, 96, 129, 185
Bodie Island Light Station 80, 209-210
Bodkin Island Light Station 29, 34
Bogus Point, New York 266
Boon Island Light Station 29, 48, 106-107
Boothbay Harbor, Maine 244
Boston Bay, Massachusetts 67
Boston Harbor Light Station 7, 8, 29, 81, 271
Boston Harbor, Massachusetts 7, 22, 67, 125, 155
Bowers Beach, Delaware 253
Braddock Point Light Station 266-267
Brandywine Shoal Light Station 78, 86, 92-94
Brant Point Light Station 58, 123
breakwater lights 193. *See also* pier lights
brick. *See* construction materials: brick
Bristol Ferry Light Station 109
Browns Head Light Station 127
brownstone. *See* construction materials: brownstone
Brunswick, Georgia 212
Buck's Harbor, Maine 102
Buffalo Harbor Light Station 29, 50-51
Buffalo Lighthouse Association 50
Bull Bay Light Station 97-98

Bullock Point Light Station  210-211
Bull's Island, South Carolina  97
buoys  172, 174, 177, 181, 254
Bureau of Lighthouses  271
Burgess, Abbie.  *See* Grant, Abbie Burgess
Burgess, Samuel  128
Burlington Bay, Minnesota  256
Burnham, Mills Olcott  194
Burnt Island Light Station  29
Burroughs, Elzy  12
Burroughs, T.  237
Buzzards Bay, Massachusetts  19, 161

C

caisson lighthouses  1, 94, 186, 187, 188, 189, 226
    pneumatic  188, 253
California Gold Rush  80, 115, 116
candles  4, 7
Cape Arago, Oregon  260
Cape Canaveral Light Station  194-195
Cape Charles Light Station  167-169
Cape Cod Bay, Massachusetts  34
Cape Cod Light Station  29, 258
Cape Cod, Massachusetts  16, 108
Cape Cod Museum of Natural History  109
Cape Cod National Seashore  259
Cape Disappointment Light Station  268
Cape Elizabeth Light Station  36, 81
Cape Elizabeth, Maine  209
Cape Flattery Light Station  129-130
Cape Florida Light Station  24, 84, 194
Cape Foulweather, Oregon  260
Cape Hatteras Light Station  29, 79, 204-205
Cape Hatteras National Seashore  205, 209
Cape Henlopen Light Station  29
Cape Henry Light Station  3, 29, 74, 237-239
Cape Mendocino Light Station  80
Cape Poge Light Station  29, 66-67
Cape Porpoise Harbor, Maine  52
Cape Romain Light Station  38, 79
Cape Romain National Wildlife Refuge  38
Cape Shoalwater Light Station.  *See* Willapa Bay Light
    Station
Cape Small Point, Maine  209
Carolina Sounds  78
Carquinez Strait Light Station  222
Carysfort Reef Light Station  24, 79, 84, 137
Casco Bay, Maine  209
cast iron.  *See* construction materials: cast iron
Cat Island Light Station  49-50
Cedar Keys Light Station  104-105
Charleston Harbor, South Carolina  214, 232
Charleston Light Station  29.  *See* Morris Island Light
    Station
Chatham Light Station  29, 63-64, 108, 258

Chatham, Massachusetts  108
Cheever, Joseph  160
Chesapeake Bay
    3, 11, 12, 34, 36, 44, 78, 110, 174, 177, 187,
    216, 226, 237
Civil War
    5, 12, 15, 23, 50, 60, 64, 83, 97, 98, 100, 105,
    106, 112, 50, 152, 168, 170, 192, 194, 196,
    209, 212, 215, 232, 250
Clarks Point Light Station  29
Cleveland Harbor East Pier Light Station  163-164
Cleveland Harbor Light Station  39-42, 125, 266
Cobb, Howell  214
cofferdams, construction with  179, 216, 224
Coffin, David  58
Cohasset, Massachusetts  159
Colfax, Harriet  148
collector of the customs.  *See* customs collectors
colonial lighthouses  1, 3, 6
Columbia River, Washington  268
Commissioner of the Revenue  5
Coney Island, New York  218
Confederate Navy  83
Confederate States Lighthouse Bureau  83
Connor, Michael  66
construction materials  1, 21, 22
    brick  1, 4, 5, 15, 21, 22, 23, 33, 34, 63, 79, 80,
      90, 97, 112, 122, 123, 127, 132, 137, 140, 152,
      160, 167, 187,  205, 206, 213, 256, 262
    brownstone  21
    cast iron  1, 22, 23, 67, 70, 108, 186, 194, 239
    concrete  1, 200, 271
    granite
      5, 14, 21, 62, 80, 88, 128, 132, 151, 159, 179,
      191, 205, 209, 216, 237, 239, 244
    iron  239
    limestone  21, 27, 50, 146, 207, 223
    rubblestone  1, 3, 5, 6, 16, 18, 19, 36, 52, 68, 100
    sandstone  11, 12, 21, 204
    steel  188, 271
    wood  1, 3, 5, 28, 58, 72, 154, 164
contractors  5, 25, 76, 77, 172, 268
Corps d'Afrique  168
Coteron, Mrs. W.E.  113
Cove Point Light Station  34-35
Craighill Channel Lower Range Light Station  216-217
Crescent City, California  257
Crescent City Light Station  103
crib construction  1, 178, 179, 224
CSS *Sumter*  83
CSS *Virginia*  12
Cumberland Island Light Station  29
custom collectors  5, 21, 25
Cutler Harbor, Maine  69
Cuttyhunk Island, Massachusetts  161
Cuttyhunk Light Station  29, 161

# T

# U

# V

# W

# Y

# Z

# About The Authors

*Nineteenth-Century Lights: Historic Images of American Lighthouses* represents the second collaboration between Candace and Mary Louise Clifford. Their first book, *Women Who Kept the Lights: An Illustrated History of Female Lighthouse Keepers*, published in 1994, enjoys continued popularity.

Candace Clifford coordinates lighthouse preservation activities for the National Park Service's National Maritime Initiative program. In addition to maintaining an inventory of light stations around the United States, she has coordinated cooperative lighthouse projects that have included the production of the *Historic Lighthouse Preservation Handbook* and creation of a lighthouse heritage web site at www.cr.nps.gov/maritime/lt_index.htm.

Mary Louise Clifford is the author of 14 books, including several introductory studies of Third World countries, social studies texts, and three novels. Her most recent book, *From Slavery to Freetown: Black Loyalists after the American Revolution*, traces the saga of American slaves freed by the British during our War for Independence, who became the founders of Freetown in West Africa.

# Lighthouse titles available from Cypress Communications

*Nineteenth-Century Lights: Historic Images of American Lighthouses*

by J. Candace Clifford and Mary Louise Clifford

Softcover (ISBN 09636412-3-9) list price $24.95 and hardcover (ISBN 09636412-2-0) list price $34.95

*Women Who Kept the Lights: An Illustrated History of Female Lighthouse Keepers*

by Mary Louise Clifford and J. Candace Clifford

Hundreds of American women have kept the lamps burning in lighthouses since Hannah Thomas tended Gurnet Point Light in Plymouth, Massachusetts, while her husband was away fighting in the War for Independence. *Women Who Kept the Lights* details the careers of 28 intrepid women who were official keepers of light stations on the Atlantic, Gulf, and Pacific Coasts, on Lake Champlain and the Great Lakes, staying at their posts for periods ranging from a decade to half a century. Most of these women served in the 19th century, when the keeper lit a number of lamps in the tower at dusk, replenished their fuel or replaced them at midnight, and every morning polished the lamps and lanterns to keep their lights shining brightly.

Originally published in 1993, *Women Who Kept the Lights: An Illustrated History of Female Lighthouse Keepers* is in its sixth printing. It is softcover (ISBN 09636412-0-4);192 pages; includes 78 illustrations, an appendix, bibliography, and index; and retails for $19.95.

*Lighthouses, Lightships, and the Gulf of Mexico*

by David L. Cipra

Eighty light stations were built on the Gulf Coast between 1811 and 1939. Shifting bars and bayous, soft and muddy bottoms, coral reefs, and periodic hurricanes challenged the skills of lighthouse designers and builders, as well as of the men and women appointed to keep the lights. Ten lightships marked the navigable waters offshore until new building techniques to overcome the many hazards were successfully engineered. Author David Cipra presents an overall survey of the shaping influences and major events of Gulf Coast history (including the Civil War), as well as the specific history of each lighthouse and lightship that has served as an aid to navigation on the coast of Texas, Louisiana, Mississippi, Alabama, and Florida.

*Lighthouses, Lightships, and the Gulf of Mexico,* 280 pages, is softcover (ISBN 09636412-1-2), retails for $24.95, and includes 93 historic photos and drawings, endnotes, bibliography, and index.

To order, make checks payable to "Cypress Communications" and send to 35 E. Rosemont Ave., Dept. B, Alexandria, VA 22301. (No shipping charges on prepaid orders.) For more information email <cypress@vais.net> or check <http://www.vais.net/~cypress>